Gypsy Spirit

What My Boat Taught Me About Love And Life

Christine M. Bukruian

Cover art from an original oil painting by S.K. Bukruian

Copyright © 2012 Christine M. Bukruian
All rights reserved.

ISBN: 1468195891
ISBN 13: 9781468195897

Gypsy Spirit is a work of nonfiction. The names of the container ship and the container ship company have been changed. The names of several individuals in the narrative have been changed to protect their identities. All others, including Ed and Kia, retain their actual names.

for my father who believed
my mother who dreamed
and Tanya who is my inspiration

You belong among the wildflowers
You belong in a boat out at sea
You belong with your love on your arm
You belong somewhere you feel free

TOM PETTY

behold your most brilliant self in the light of your darkest hour

CMB

Contents

Gypsy Spirit Returns

September 2006

Oasis Boatyard
Saint Augustine, Florida

I looked in the mirror, tilted my head this way and that, and for the first time in months, thought—I like what I see. The eyes smiling back at me sparkled, and there was a healthy glow in my cheeks. I turned off the faucet, dried my hands, and stepped back out into the bright sun. It was getting harder to contain my excitement, and on impulse I poked my head into Nancy's office…again. She looked up, smiled then shook her head in answer to my unspoken question.

I resumed pacing the landing. Finally after what seemed like forever, there it was—very faint at first, nothing more than a low rumble; the ground trembled ever so slightly… but I knew—my boat was near at last. I waited as *Gypsy Spirit* lumbered painfully over pothole and rut down Riberia Street, and then watched as the tractor trailer carrying my battered, beaten boat reached the gate and turned into Oasis Boatyard. It rumbled across the crushed gravel, raising a cloud of dust, then came to an abrupt stop.

A moment later the travel lift appeared like a giant spider with long gangly legs; John maneuvered the vehicle into place, and carefully lifted my boat from the trailer, then set her front and center by Nancy's office, in the spot that would become my home. Five months had passed since the accident; three since I last saw my boat; and now here she was. I stepped forward and placed my palm against the hull.

"You're home, *Gypsy Spirit*," I whispered.

Uncertain of what I would find, I climbed the ladder and stepped gingerly into the cockpit. Noting the damaged teak and shattered fiberglass, I slid open the hatch and peered down into the darkness. Leaning forward just a bit to get a better look, I gagged as the stench of decay wafted up from the cabin. After the initial burst of fetid air, I risked another glance and discovered the culprit. My inflatable, having spent months half submerged in the polluted water of Luperon harbor, now sat below deck—with all its mud, funk, and animal life—marinating. A slimy film of rancid grey ooze coated every visible surface.

What had I gotten myself into? Maybe I should have listened to all the naysayers. Carefully, avoiding the muck, I climbed down into the boat then moved through the galley toward my cabin. The room looked eerily as I'd left it months ago: a coverlet folded on the bunk, a pair of flip flops on the floor, a few DVDs and knickknacks on the shelf. I opened the portlights and a fresh breeze wafted through the cabin. I climbed onto the bunk, and peeked out into the main salon toward the bookshelves that were still intact, and it almost seemed that it hadn't happened. Tears threatened, as they did so often lately. I laid my head upon the pillow, just as I had every night for more than a year, and I was home; even in that condition, broken and rancid, *Gypsy Spirit* was my home.

Christening Gypsy Spirit

Living The Dream

May 2005

Municipal Marina
Saint Augustine, Florida

For as long as I could remember, I'd dreamed of living on a boat and falling asleep to the gentle swoosh and sway of the ocean; I dreamed of becoming a sea gypsy and taking my home with me as I travelled from port to port. I didn't know much about boats when I bought the old sailing sloop, *Manatee*, and renamed her *Gypsy Spirit*. Maybe things would have turned out differently had I known that it was bad luck to rename a boat, but sometimes you just have to close your eyes, hold your breath, and jump. And that's what I did. I bought an old boat, christened her *Gypsy Spirit*, put my house on the market, and cajoled my reluctant fifty-pound mutt, Kia, into moving aboard.

In the beginning I counted the days by the number of bruises I'd acquired learning to live and work in tight quarters. My knowledge of boats was limited to the brief tutorial Rick from Polaris had given on the workings of my Perkins 4-108 diesel engine. He'd pointed out all the major components and described their function. He'd also given me a copy of the shop manual. Aside from that most of the boat's systems, mechanical or otherwise, were a complete mystery. So although I was anxious to sail away into the blue, I knew it would be several months before I was ready.

I'd been living aboard for almost a week, and everything was coming along nicely. The cabin woodwork gleamed, but I still had a lot to do to make the boat a home. From the smell of it, replacing the old head was a definite priority— no need to consult the growing to-do list to figure that one out. My friends Rob and Beth, who'd just sold their own boat, offered to help. Beth, being a woman and thereby the smarter of the sexes, lent her support by offering me her husband. Rob, poor Rob, he actually got right in there and, as we coined it, *became one with the shit*.

As Rob struggled to remove the odiferous steel-reinforced rubber hose that had carried almost thirty years' worth of waste from the head to the holding tank, I stayed close by, watching and handing him tools. A few times, when his own hands wouldn't fit, he had me reach into a tight spot. But mostly I commiserated. If he had to breathe the stench, then I would breathe it right along with him. When he turned to look at me, I was careful to make sure my face reflected appropriate degrees of sympathy and concern. I wanted him to know that I felt his pain and, believe me, I did—I really did.

"Having fun yet?" he asked, when we stopped to bag several sections of slimy, muck-encrusted hose.

"I'm living the dream. It's everything I imagined...and *so* much more," I answered with a laugh, not wanting to complain and undermine how grateful I was for his help.

"You *are* living the dream, and I'm a bit envious. I remember what it was like," Rob said wistfully. "Just wait. You're going to love life aboard ship."

"I know I will, and I do already. It's great, but I've never felt so helpless and...useless."

"We all need help sometimes, and with a boat, there's a huge learning curve. You'll do fine; stop worrying."

Several hours of oozing sludge later, we were almost ready to install the new head. Rob sighed and lifted the old toilet. There were smudges on his cheeks and forehead, and nasty pink welts ran down the lengths of his forearms. I hadn't known what a horrendous job this would be, and he'd gone far beyond the call of friendship. When had he last had a tetanus shot?

"Here, let me get that," I said, reaching to take the porcelain bowl from him. I proceeded awkwardly up the ladder and was just about to step onto the dock when I heard my neighbor Sam calling.

"Christine, there you are. I want you to meet my friend... the sailor I told you about."

Lovely, just what I needed. Sam's timing definitely wasn't great. Actually it *stunk* almost as bad as what I held in my arms. Since the day Sam first introduced himself, he'd taken to popping in often and unexpectedly. He lived three boats down from me, aboard his sailboat, *Emotional Rescue,* about which he'd written a memoir called *A Sail and a Tale of an Emotional Rescue.*

The day we met, Sam told me of his Greek heritage and his life in the fast lane; he told me how he'd made and lost a fortune, battled cancer, and suffered an emotional breakdown. He'd shared all of this within ten minutes of our meeting and initially, I didn't know whether to be concerned or amused, but he was kind, especially to Kia, bringing her dog treats and taking her for walks. Sam missed his own dog, who now resided with ex-wife number three. Several days prior, during one of his impromptu visits, he mentioned a friend who'd sailed across the Atlantic from South Africa. The friend would be passing through Saint Augustine soon, and Sam wanted us to meet.

But why did it have to be now? My hair was falling into my eyes, and I could barely see. I balanced the toilet on the lifelines and used the back of a grimy hand to push several strands aside, and then I lifted the toilet and pivoted trying to get it off the boat and into a dock cart, but Sam was blocking my way. Sticky, sweating, and feeling more than a bit peeved, the last thing I wanted to do was exchange pleasantries. I glared at Sam with what my daughter calls *the death stare* until the *friend* obligingly pulled Sam back enough to give me access to the dock.

"Thanks," I mumbled and couldn't help notice how attractive he was, in an earthy-crunchy, singlehanded sailor, I-don't-care-to-brush-my-hair sort of way. He was tall, six foot something; he stood at least a head over Sam and was looking down at me with what I perceived to be a mixture of amusement and curiosity. He had his chin-length, sun-streaked hair tied back, and his azure blue eyes shone large against the raccoon white rings left by his sunglasses. I had somehow imagined that the friend would be a sixty-something replica of Sam, not a *Captain Ron* look-alike.

Suddenly self-conscious I performed a quick mental inventory: dirty, rumpled peasant skirt, slime-stained tank top, hair clipped in a messy heap at the top of my head, sweat and I don't know what else covering almost every inch of exposed skin. He'd probably say a polite hello and move on; then I could get back to work.

He didn't. He just stood there watching me, not saying a word—and I don't like being watched. For years I'd practiced and considered myself an expert on the art of invisibility. Some people enjoy the spotlight; I am not one of them. I prefer quietly observing from a safe distance. How else does one manage to move about under male radar? Thankfully, but after what seemed like forever, Sam broke the silence.

"This is my good friend Ed; he sailed here from South Africa aboard his boat, *Nini*."

I hoisted the filthy toilet into the dock cart, wiped my hand on my skirt, and reached out. Ed glanced almost imperceptibly at my hand and raised an eyebrow. The smile in his eyes spread to his lips and then he took my hand firmly in his.

"Hello."

"Hi." I smiled totally flustered. "Sam has mentioned quite a bit about you."

"Ya, I'm sure he has."

I was dumbstruck. Perhaps he was simply stating a fact, but the way he said it, with that accent and the lazy smile playing about his lips, the man seemed downright arrogant.

"Well, gentlemen, this has been fun, and Ed it was really nice to meet you. But as you can see, I'm kind of in the middle of something, and I..."

Rob chose that moment to pop his head up from the companionway.

"How's it going up here? Do you need any help with—oh, hi—I didn't realize you had company."

"Oh, no, not company. This is Sam. You guys met the other day. Remember?"

"Hey, Sam." Rob nodded in greeting.

"And this is Ed. He's an *old* sailor friend of Sam's." I gestured vaguely in Ed's direction.

"Nice to meet you," Rob said, and they shook.

"Rob is helping me replace the head," I said. "Actually, he's replacing the head. I'm just watching."

"That's not true; we're in this together. We've become one with the shit," Rob said, and we laughed.

"You had to be there," I explained. Then noting Sam's confused look and Ed's raised eyebrow I changed the subject. "Ed sailed here from South Africa; he's on his way to the Bahamas."

"Well, there you go. You wanted stories," Rob said. Then looking at Ed for confirmation, he continued, "I bet you have lots of sailing stories?"

"Actually—not so many," he replied in an off-handed manner.

I was overcome with an intense urge to accidentally bump Ed off the dock and watch the self-satisfied look go overboard with him.

But instead I smiled placidly and said,"Well, listen, we really need to get back to work. We've got a toilet to install, and Rob has to leave soon."

"Okay, we'll get out of your hair—just wanted you two to meet. We're heading over to Tradewinds for a drink. Maybe see you later on?" Sam said.

"Sounds good," I said watching them walk away.

Out of the corner of my eye I caught Rob's expression.

"What?" I asked.

He smiled and shrugged.

"What?" I repeated.

"Looks like someone *likes* you," he teased.

"What? Him? No...he's Sam's friend. Sam wanted us to meet. Why? Did it seem like he liked me?" I asked.

"Well, yeah...and I think I saw a bit of a twinkle in your eye."

"A twinkle? In my eye? I don't think so..."

"No?"

"No...No! Actually, I thought he was rude...and annoying and really arrogant. Didn't you think he was rude?"

Do you think I was born yesterday? Rob's penetrating gaze seemed to ask, but then he said, "I guess so. Let's get back to work. Why don't you invite your new friend along to dinner next week? Beth would be thrilled to meet someone who sailed across the Atlantic," he said and started towards the dumpster with the dock cart.

"He's not *my friend*...but if you think Beth would enjoy his company..."

I stretched lazily, unable to imagine anything more perfect than lying in my gently swaying berth enjoying the soft breeze and morning sunshine. It was all coming together; I now had running water and a working head; other than learning how to actually operate my boat, what more could I ask for? Even Kia seemed disinclined to move—no cold wet nose prodding me to take her for a walk. I smiled...A year ago, even six months ago, who would have believed we'd actually be here: on a boat, turning a dream into reality, about to embark on the adventure of a lifetime. I wished my mom could have been here; she loved adventure; she was going to fix her old VW camper, Buttercup, and travel the country, maybe go to Mexico. She was going to open a bakery and write a book...She had so many dreams—a dozen lifetimes wouldn't have been enough or maybe...I felt the now familiar, breathless dull pain in my gut that came each time I remembered that she was gone. Just then there came a not so tentative *rap tap tap* on the hull; I stood and popped my head out through the hatch.

"Wow..." Ed said incredulously, as I blinked in the bright morning sunlight. "Still sleeping; half the day is gone."

"I wasn't sleeping." What did my hair look like? I was sure it was sticking up and out in every direction, but, not wanting to give him the satisfaction, I resisted the urge and let it be. "I've been awake for hours. I was just resting, enjoying the breeze."

"Uh-huh…Well, in that case, don't let me disturb your…rest," he said, then turned as if to leave.

"Don't go. Come on aboard. I was just about to make coffee."

"If you're making—don't do it just for me," he said with a shrug. "I'm supposed to take a look at Sam's engine, but he's still sleeping too."

"I wasn't sleeping. I…" I noticed his smile. "Never mind."

I hopped out of my bunk and peered in the mirror, then combed my fingers through a few unruly locks. I put the coffee on to brew, brushed my teeth, splashed my face, and made a second brief attempt to tame my hair, which had gone from straight to curly in the Florida humidity.

"While the coffee brews, I'm going to take Kia for a walk. Want to come?" I asked, stepping off the boat onto the dock. "C'mon Kia, let's go."

"I hear you're going cruising soon," Ed said as we walked together toward the grassy patch by the side of the marina.

"Not that soon. It will take at least a month to get the boat ready, then I have to learn how to motor. Hopefully we'll head out in August. My daughter, Tanya, and her boyfriend are coming with me for the first few months; she's taking a semester off from college."

"Where are you heading?" Ed asked.

"The Keys. After that I'm not sure…somewhere south."

"Hmm…I see," he responded.

"What do you see?" I asked, starting to feel defensive.

"Everything; but no matter."

"Kia, come on, pup, back to the boat. Good girl."

She came bounding over, tail wagging. I was happy with how quickly she'd settled into life at the marina.

As we reached the boat, Ed continued, "So you were saying...something about heading south—in the middle of hurricane season."

"What? I didn't say anything about hurricane season."

"I know...never mind—just something I was thinking."

"Oh, okay, whatever...Are you ready for coffee?" I asked.

"Yes, please."

"How do you take it?"

"Three spoons sugar and milk."

"How much milk?"

"Enough."

"How much is enough?

"Till it's nice. By the way, does your engine work?"

"Yeah, why?" I asked absently, trying to decide how much milk would make it "nice."

"Sam tells me you've had the boat here for a month and haven't left the slip. I thought maybe you were having engine problems."

"No. The plan is to get all the work done and then worry about learning to sail," I said and handed up the coffee.

"Thanks. I see..." he repeated.

"Again with the 'I see.' What do you see?"

"Why can't you learn to sail while you fix the boat?" he asked and tentatively sipped the coffee.

"I need to learn how to dock first and how to motor around. I'll worry about the actual sailing part later. I talked to the dockmaster about finding someone to teach me.

Ed looked confused. "You can't learn to sail because you can't get in and out of the slip?"

"Sort of," I responded defensively.

"Why don't we solve that problem right now?" he suggested.

"Now. You? You're going to teach me? No…I couldn't… and besides, you're busy. I wouldn't…and also I'd feel bad. Sam's been offering, but…you know…and I don't want to hurt his feelings. A lot of people have offered actually. I'm just not…"

"Wow. Do you want to do this or not? Sam won't be up for at least another hour. We'll take her out, motor around a bit, and bring her back. We can go out again later with Sam if that will make you feel better."

"If you're sure, then, yeah, sounds good. We'll finish our coffee and take her out for a bit."

Kia sat in the cockpit, alert and watchful. She knew something different was about to happen, and she wasn't quite sure yet whether she liked it or not.

"What should I do?" I asked.

"Whatever you want…take the helm or cast off."

I hesitated for a second, trying to decide which option had the least potential for screwing up. "I'll drive."

Ed stood and looked around, checking wind direction and current, mentally planning our exit from the slip.

"I'm going to untie the lines starting there," he said, pointing to the stern and midship dock lines. "Then I'll untie the bow line, guide the boat out, and jump on. Hold the wheel straight till I say, then turn it all the way to the left…Got it?"

I nodded—tense, but ready. He untied the lines, and with a smooth leap, he was on the deck.

"Should I turn?" My heart was beating loud and fast. I tried to project a look of calm control as I maneuvered the vessel out into the channel.

"Not yet," he said quietly, coiling the dock lines as he watched our progress. He was at ease; I tried to relax and drew in a deep breath, then exhaled. "Keep going…a little bit more…more…okay; now…*turn*…*turn!* I said *turn!*"

"I am, nothing's happening, the wheel just spins!" Everything seemed to be happening so fast and in slow motion all at the same time.

"*Move,*" he commanded, then took my place at the helm and spun the wheel first left then right. "Your steering cable's snapped."

"I'll throw out the anchor," I said and scrambled to the bow.

"No, not yet." He looked astern, the direction we were heading, toward the pier and the Santa Maria Restaurant.

"We're gonna hit the restaurant! Maybe I should throw the anchor out."

"No. Not yet, hold on." He was completely absorbed, shifting back and forth from reverse to forward, and slowly the boat began turning away from the restaurant's pilings. Back and forth—a bit in reverse, then forward. Each time he shifted, the boat turned, bit by bit till he was able to get us into a clearing.

"Okay, you can drop that anchor now."

I let loose the anchor in a quick motion. Ed came and took the rope from my hand, cleated it off, waited, let out more, and cleated it off again. The line tightened like a rubber band, then went slack.

"I'm sorry," I said.

"Sorry for what?" He looked at me perplexed.

"For this. Here you are trying to help me, and now *this*."

"*This* is part of sailing," he replied.

"Oh! You know what?" I said as inspiration struck. "I just remembered something; don't worry. I have TowBoat US. I'll give them a call."

"You have TowBoat US," he repeated.

"Yes, don't you know what it is?" I asked, figuring that they didn't have TowBoat US in South Africa. "You call and they come and get you, like triple-A." I started down the companionway to retrieve my cell phone and make the call.

"Ya...listen, hold on," Ed drawled in that Afrikans accent that I was really beginning to enjoy.

"What?" I asked while rummaging for the phone.

"I'm not a TowBoat US kind of guy," he stated.

Now it was my turn to repeat. "You're not a TowBoat US kind of guy. Um, okay...what kind of guy are you?"

"I'm the fix it myself kind," he said nonchalantly.

"The fix it yourself kind...you mean you can fix the steering?"

"I should be able to."

"Oh, okay. By the way, how did you get the boat to turn like that?"

"Prop walk," he replied. "You can read all about it in the book I brought over. The other three books will fascinate you as well." He pointed to a small stack of books in the cockpit that I hadn't noticed earlier.

"I wouldn't feel right having you fix the steering. I can't pay you. I'd really rather have the boat towed in."

"Make me lunch. That will be payment enough," he suggested.

"No, that wouldn't be fair."

"All right then, lunch and dinner," he continued.

I laughed. "All right, you win—lunch and dinner." I didn't want to admit, even to myself, how much I was looking forward to spending the day with this oddly endearing stranger. I felt my face get warm as I imagined Rob's I-told-you-so reaction.

"Woman, stop daydreaming. Let's get on the radio and get a hold of Sam. I need tools and my dinghy, and you need to make a run for parts."

We hailed Sam, who after his initial consternation at having his two friends "sneak off" without him, rose to the occasion and ferried Ed ashore to retrieve his dinghy. Ed returned and began dismantling the steering pedestal.

"Okay, we're going to need some cable, the type you use for rigging—and see these links?" He handed me a few links of what appeared to be bicycle chain. "We need some of this." He removed the existing broken cable. "You can take this with you and just get the same thing. I'll be waiting at the dock."

Ed fixed the steering system, quietly, methodically, pausing from time to time when something was stuck, but never getting frustrated or impatient. It was a pleasure watching him work, and as the afternoon passed, I became aware of how unusually comfortable I felt with this man that I barely knew. Perhaps it was his focus…all his energy directed toward the task. I watched his hands, fingers long and graceful, working unobtrusively, deftly guiding cable, handling tools and hardware. This was a patient man, I decided, a man who didn't lose his cool even in emergencies. This was a man one could trust, and it had been a long time since I'd trusted anyone.

I was sitting, wedged underneath the large cushion that was my mattress, using my back to hold it up and give Ed access to the steering quadrant below. He had already run the new cables to the quadrant and was fastening them in place with cable clamps.

"Could you pass me a spanner?" he asked.

"A spanner?"

"*Wrench.*"

"Weren't you nervous?" I asked and handed him the wrench.

"Hmm...when?"

"When we lost steering."

"Yes, I was."

"That was you nervous?" I asked.

"That was me very nervous," he answered.

"I was jumping all over the place; I wanted to throw the anchor out."

"You were reacting, and that will get you in trouble. Always look, think, and then *act*—never react."

I thought of the expression; *when the student is ready, the teacher appears.*

Ed came back the next day and the next. His stay of a few days turned into a few weeks; May turned to June; I felt as though this was the only life I'd ever known, and Ed had always been there. We'd start each day with coffee on my boat and then move on to some boat-related task. Evenings would inevitably find us chitchatting over coffee.

"So you're from Boston?" Ed asked one night.

"Uh-huh."

"What made you decide to buy a boat and move aboard?"

I shrugged. "My mom. She passed away last year, about a week before my daughter's high school graduation; she'd been sick for a few years, but it still came as a shock. Our last conversation changed my life."

Ed waited for me to continue.

"She said, 'Chris, I can't die. I haven't lived my dreams. I thought there would be more time.'" I paused to collect myself. "I felt so helpless; I hugged her, but there was nothing else I could do. Two days later the call came. I felt so angry and numb and invincible."

Ed raised an eyebrow. "Invincible?"

"Yeah, but not what you think. It was like I had nothing to lose, the worst that could possibly have happened did...So there was nothing left to be afraid of. And there was this urgency—I had to keep moving. I loaded the car and took off: no plans, no responsibilities, no business, no bills; for once in my life, I didn't care what anyone thought. I drove and drove until I ended up in Key West."

"And then?" Ed asked.

I thought about the catamaran ride from Key West to Dry Tortuga. The boat had carried about a hundred passengers, but I was traveling alone. It was my birthday, and if my mom couldn't be there, I didn't want to be with anyone. I'd stood at the bow with the wind and sun on my face as the boat glided through the sea, and I'd felt her presence. She had loved the ocean. For that moment I was at peace, and it was then that I knew I wouldn't go back to my old life; I had to seek out and live my dreams.

"Hello? Is there anybody in there?" Ed asked, waving a hand in front of my eyes.

"Oh. What was I saying?"

"You said you went to Key West, and…"

"Right, I took a boat ride and decided to buy a boat and then I moved to Saint Augustine."

"And your family was okay with this."

"Are you kidding? My dad was so upset; he cancelled his trip to Florida. He said it was the biggest mistake I'd ever made in my life. He's gotten over it, though." I smiled and added, "And Tanya's excited, you know, for our trip."

"Sounds like a plan," Ed said.

"Well, what about you? How did you end up cruising?"

"Not as exciting as your story."

"I'd like to hear," I said and smiled.

"We wanted to travel—my girlfriend Sofie and I—before we ended up married with kids and jobs and a mortgage. But we knew if we flew, we'd just end up stuck somewhere else working to pay the rent. So we decided to buy a boat and take our home with us."

"Makes sense…When did you learn to sail?" I asked, imagining he'd always been a sailor.

"During the two years we spent paying off the mortgage on the boat; we sailed a lot on weekends, but really it was during the trip across the Atlantic."

"You learned to sail during the crossing!"

"We had three weeks with nothing to do but play with sail trim, and we had Johan."

"Johan?"

"A friend of a friend—a captain who helped us with the crossing."

"Oh, there were three of you."

"Ya, but Sofie got pretty sick. She was ill for most of the crossing."

"That sucks. I can't imagine being stuck on a boat for weeks if I were sick. What happened—you guys aren't together anymore?"

"No, we cruised for a few years, but she got tired of the life. She missed her family and wanted to go home. It was the best thing really…for her. We were together for fourteen years, though. Hey, don't they say you shouldn't talk about one woman when you're with another?"

"Yes *they* do say that, but don't worry, I asked. I just think it's sad that you're not together after all that time; you must miss her."

"Are you trying to depress me? She left in February; this is the longest we've been apart." At my look, he added, "I still feel like we're together, and we talk every week."

"Tell me about the crossing," I asked a few days later. "What was it like? Was it scary?"

"You want to know the truth?"

"Yes." I imagined he was about to tell me of the storms they'd weathered and how they barely made it alive.

"You might find it rather disappointing."

"Yeah right, come on. Tell me."

"Well, basically, we could have set our sails, flown to Brazil, and met the boat there a month later."

"What?"

"That's it. We set out with the trade winds. Days would pass without even having to adjust the sails. I started messing around with sail trim out of boredom. I read a lot. Like I told you, Sofie was pretty sick the whole way, but other than that nothing happened."

"Hmm…"

"Bit of a letdown, huh?"

"Actually, no, it isn't." Rather than finding his tale boring, I found it comforting. Irrationally, it furthered my faith in him, as though he were responsible for the calm weather and smooth crossing.

He told me about his adventures in the Bahamas, where the water was so clear you could see the ripples on the ocean floor, and dolphins swam up to say hello. And the fish—there were fish by the hundreds in every shape and color. The islands were of course deserted—swaying palms and white sand as far as you could see. I loved listening to those stories.

"It sounds amazing. I wish I were going now instead of August."

"What's stopping you?" he asked.

"I'm not ready." I felt an odd stirring in the pit of my stomach.

"What do you need to do?"

"Everything. And then learn how to handle my boat."

"The best way to learn is to untie those dock lines and do it. As far as fixing things, we can take care of everything as we go."

"We?" I asked, unsure I heard correctly.

"Ya, I don't see that there's anything we couldn't handle along the way."

"I get that. But you just said *we*. Are you asking me to come with you?"

"There isn't going to be any better time. At least now I'd be there to help if you got into a tight spot."

"But I don't know what I'm doing. It would be a huge responsibility for you."

"And for you."

"Yeah, I know, but I don't want to become a burden. You've already spent so much time fixing my boat and teaching me things."

"What else would I be doing? Besides, you're helping me too."

"I am? How?" I asked.

"You give me purpose. I enjoy sharing what I've learned."

I smiled, happy that I had something to give, even if it was only my inexperience and desire to learn.

"I'd need weeks to get ready."

"Maybe not. If we hustle—I mean work from morning to night—we could be ready in about ten days."

"That would mean more of a delay for you. And I thought you were leaving in a day or so." I reminded, giving him an opportunity to back out.

"Ya, me too, and it's already been three weeks—another two won't make that much difference."

"Ed, don't ask unless you really mean it—because I might just say yes."

"I guess we'd better get to work. By the way, can I see that famous to-do list of yours?"

"Sure. Why?"

"Just curious."

I went below, opened my journal, pulled out the tattered list, and passed it up to him. There was silence for a moment, then laughter—or perhaps he was choking.

"What's so funny?" I asked innocently.

"I wouldn't say funny. Actually, it's terrifying…

To Do

~~*Replace head*~~
make curtains
fix water pressure
attach toilet paper holder
sew fitted sheets
make bookshelves
buy matching bedding
~~*varnish interior woodwork*~~
mattress pads
raincoat for Kia
~~*throw rugs*~~
new journal
placemats and napkins
buy small dish rack"

He finished reading, and then looked at me as if trying to decide if this were some sick joke. "This is the list. This is what needs to be done for your boat to be ready?" he asked.

"Uh-huh. And maybe a few other things. Why?" I asked with the best awaiting-enlightenment expression I could muster.

"Curtains! Placemats! Throw rugs! What kind of drugs are you on? You know what…never mind. Pass me a pen." He began writing furiously, adding to my list, muttering as he went.

"repair soft spot on deck under mast
add second reef to mainsail
fix roller-furler bearing
weld steering wheel
replace main and jib sheets
safety netting
check rigging
GPS
dinghy and outboard
50 feet 3/8ths chain
additional line
spare fuel and oil filters
spare anchor
spark plugs
fuel and water jugs
emergency ditch bag
read books on boat handling,
heavy weather tactics, navigation…"

"And when you've read those, I'll give you a few more."

Now it was my turn to be dumbstruck. I was vaguely aware that certain items needed addressing, *vaguely* being the key word. Even if I had put those items on my list, I wouldn't have known where to start. My idea of fixing a soft spot on the deck was to take the boat to a boatyard, but I didn't have, *take-it-to-the-boatyard,* resources. And exactly how did one go about fixing a roller-furler bearing? What on earth was a roller-furler bearing?

"And the hound…" He pet Kia as he spoke. "Check the requirements: she may need vaccines, and you have to get a permit. You're going to have to teach her to go to the bathroom on deck. There will be times when we can't get to shore."

Rebuilding The Dream

October 2006

Oasis Boatyard
Saint Augustine, Florida

I removed the blue tape at my wrists and peeled away my coveralls—carefully, so as not to raise the fine dust that always managed to find a way into my ears and nose and eyes. Exhausted, I sank to the ground beside my boat. At least I no longer hurt in ways that made me question my sanity on a daily basis, and I'd finally gathered the courage to cut into the hull and remove most of the cracked and damaged area. I looked up at the large egg-shaped orifice about eighteen inches wide and three feet high and marveled, not for the first time, that I hadn't sunk that night out on the sea. Kia noticed that I'd stopped to rest and came bounding over from the office to say hello. She'd taken to spending workdays with Nancy, either in Nancy's air-conditioned office or on the porch where she could keep an eye on me. I scratched the silky fur around her ears for a moment then stopped. She nudged my arm urging me to continue.

"What is it pup?" I asked as I scratched her lower back and hip. Kia leaned against me her face a reflection of pure bliss. "What would I do without you girl?" We sat quietly together beside the boat, two old friends, like a book and its cover, until I noticed that the boatyard had woken from its lunchtime slumber "I have to get back to work, pup. Why don't you go see Nancy." I scratched her ears one last time before she got up and trotted off towards the office.

I was now quite proficient in the use of power tools; the grinder in particular, which frightened me initially, had practically become an appendage. It was my new best friend, allowing me to remove large areas of damaged and delaminated rock-hard fiberglass and resin. Eight hours a day, five days a week, my grinder hummed. I'd been at it so long I could feel the vibration under my skin, reverberating in the muscle and sinew, even as I lay in bed at night.

While my body fought to restore the ruined hull, my mind waged war with demons of its own; there was too much time to think, to replay the moments leading up to the accident... to ask what I could have or should have or might have done differently.

Daily I questioned why I was doing this, why I hadn't simply used the settlement money and bought another boat like everyone suggested—surely there was one out there somewhere. Did I even want to sail again? Would I sail again? The answers depended on the time of day and sometimes even the weather; but then I would remember how I had felt, returning to Boston without my boat…

The first few days had been great, and I was happy to see everyone. I moved in with my childhood friend Marina, who'd always been like a big sister to me, but life in the suburbs soon left me feeling slightly catatonic. I missed the boat and Ed and our adventures on the water. My family and friends couldn't relate; they wanted me to "snap out of it" and "get back to normal," but what was "normal"? I didn't know anymore. I struggled to redefine myself; I was no longer a sailor, no longer Gypsy Spirit cruising with Nini. I was a woman with a wreck of a boat who'd traded in all her worldly possessions for a dream, and I was slowly but surely falling into a dreamless sleep. My body functioned, and I went through all the motions of day-to-day life, but I wasn't really there. I drifted through days then weeks in a fog—the only light being the weekly phone calls from Ed. Find a boat, he urged, we'll go sailing again. He wasn't happy either; each week he told me how tempted he was to just pack up and head to Boston. Deep in my heart, I harbored a glimmer of hope that I'd arrive at work one day, and he'd be there. But it didn't happen, and time passed. One day he called.

"You should come," I urged, upon hearing how unhappy he was.

"I know. I keep thinking—we were good together—everyone thought we were a couple. Sometimes I think—we should just sail away together. We get along really well; problem is… I'm not in love with you."

He needn't have said anymore. Although he continued to speak and tried to elaborate, I neither remember nor heard another word." In an instant, the impenetrable wall materialized, stronger than ever—as if it had never been breached—and I felt so very comfortably and completely numb.

I passed the days trying to do normal things, like grow my business, which had been neglected since my mom passed, and I looked for a boat. I looked at so many, but none compared to *Gypsy Spirit*. In my opinion they weren't built strong enough or crafted well enough—they lacked space and function. I graded each boat on whether it would have survived the collision, and each came up lacking. My Watkins 36 might have been a tub, but with her massive aluminum toe rails and extra thick hull, she'd seen us through that night and I credited her for our survival.

And so the weeks passed until one day on a trip to the supermarket, I noticed a solitary miniature rosebush sitting in soil so dry that the plant lifted easily from the pot and the blossoms, not yet unfurled, were shriveled and dropping from the frail spider web-like branches; it was the one that got left behind, and my heart broke for the helpless flower. How much longer would this plant survive with the approach of fall and lack of water? And then, out of nowhere, another thought: how much longer would my boat survive out there alone—in a remote Dominican village? I pushed the nagging thought aside.

I had to rescue the plant. That much I knew for sure. I reached out and gently lifted it from the shelf, and as I did so, two months of inertia magically evaporated. The light seemed suddenly brighter; the produce smelled fresher, sweeter; it was as though in that instant my world had turned from black-and-white to color. Marina glanced over from the berry section and saw me holding the plant. She shook her head—then shifted her gaze back to the blueberries, pointed at the placard, and said, "See. Or-gan-ic," as if trying to find the magic words to bring me back.

"Marina…I know what I'm going to do. I'm going to bring *Gypsy Spirit* home; I'm going to rebuild her."

I flipped the power switch and the grinder whirred to life. Two weeks into the restoration and I knew one thing for sure: *Gypsy Spirit* would sail again. And, hopefully somewhere along the way, I would find the bits of myself that had been lost. I tried to stay focused on the task, imagining the boat finished, hull gleaming in whatever color I chose; and then Ed and I sailing together again…as friends. Mostly though, I passed the time remembering. Like a favorite movie, I replayed cherished scenes over and over, and the hours slipped by.

Like a deer in the headlights...Departure day

The Adventure Begins

June 2005

Intercoastal Waterway
Florida

We worked tirelessly from sunrise to sunset, and I could now recognize most of the miscellaneous bits and pieces at Sailor's Exchange, the secondhand boat shop that we frequented at least once a day. Ed repaired the soft spot on the fore deck, and I learned a bit about working with fiberglass and resin. When we weren't working, I was reading about boat handling and sail trim. Our conversations became quizzes on anchoring techniques and foul-weather tactics. The only thing I lacked was practical experience, and that was soon to come.

In a matter of hours, we would set sail for destinations unknown, for sunshine and blue skies, turquoise water and pink sand beaches. My new life had just begun, and I wanted to remember every stress-filled wonderful second. It was still dark when I climbed out onto the dock, but along the horizon the inky blackness gave way to a pale grey, and the rising sun seemed to bathe my boat in a halo of light. I snapped several photos before going back inside to make coffee. The morning passed in a blur of restless slow motion until Ed arrived. I surprised him with a little birthday celebration: two cupcakes and a couple of Dr. Seuss books. And then it was time to leave; We'd decided to move my boat to the anchorage and wait there until the tide was favorable. Ed took the helm; I undid the dock lines. We fueled the boat, then anchored just behind *Nini*. Ed said he had some last minute details to take care of and stepped down into his dinghy.

"Give me about an hour, then come over if you like."

"Oh, no, that's okay. I'll just hang here." I wasn't comfortable with the dinghy, hadn't quite mastered using a tiller.

"On second thought, I'll come and get you."

"Sure…sounds great, thanks."

Alone, I began questioning my sanity. What had I been thinking? I wasn't prepared for this. In less than two hours, I'd be pulling up the anchor and handling my thirty-six-foot, seventeen-thousand-pound boat…alone. Had this ever seemed appealing, it certainly didn't now. I felt ill. Granted, I'd read a great deal, and Ed and I had talked boat-handling incessantly for weeks. But would that be enough? Would I be able to weigh anchor and then manage to get back to the cockpit in time to steer away from other boats? Most importantly, why on earth was I doing this? Suddenly I couldn't remember.

Kia announced Ed's return by thumping her tail vigorously against the side of the cabin before jumping into his dinghy with get-me-out-of-here enthusiasm. Although I tried to hide my nervousness, she was a barometer reflecting my emotional state. She glanced up at me with a wag of encouragement that said "come on, escape is at hand!"

Taking her cue, I scurried down and onto the pontoon across from Ed. The outboard revved to life, and moments later, Kia and I were seated side by side aboard *Nini*. I sat mutely, wishing now that we were taking this trip with Ed, on his boat, as Sam had suggested. I heard a click and looked up.

"For posterity," Ed said. He turned the digital camera in my direction to show me the photo. I had to laugh as the phrase "deer in the headlights" came to mind.

"Can you do me a favor?" Ed asked. "I haven't had a chance, but it's really important."

"Sure," I replied, not sure of anything but not wanting to refuse after all he'd done for me. "What do you need?"

"This chain," he said, moving to the bow and pointing to a mound of rusted chain. "We need to clean the rust off."

I couldn't imagine why it was so important to clean the chain now. He handed me a wire brush and two buckets of salt water. After a brief explanation, he disappeared.

"So much for *we,*" I mumbled to no one in particular; then fed a length of chain into the first bucket, held it against the side, scrubbed a bit, and rinsed it in the second bucket. There must have been at least a hundred feet. I sighed and looked at Kia; I could have sworn she was snickering. After the first twenty feet or so, I found the rhythm: brush brush, shlop shlop, brush brush, shlop shlop. It was oddly cathartic, watching the rust disappear under my brush. I understood then what it meant to be present in what you are doing. I thought of the Karate Kid and Mr. Miagi. At that moment I was very present.

"Feeling better?" Ed's voice cut in.

"Actually, yes. Why?"

"No reason, just thought you seemed less nervous," he said. I wondered briefly if he'd purposely set me to this task. I was beginning to suspect that there was a motive to everything Ed did or said, but surely I was being paranoid.

He pulled the dinghy up close to the boat, and my brief respite was over. I climbed down and called Kia.

"Come on, girl, let's go." She looked at me suspiciously, head down, neck level with her back. I could almost hear her saying "I don't think so…" I understood her misgivings; they mirrored my own.

"I'm going to pull up my anchor first," Ed said. "The tide's slack, so it shouldn't be so bad."

"Okay" was all I could manage as I climbed onto my boat and reached down to pull Kia aboard; Ed pushed from below. "Come on, girl, you can do it," I urged. "Ed, we have to figure something out…maybe a step, so that I can get her up without your help."

"Listen," he said as he stood holding the side of my boat, "everyone gets nervous in the beginning. It's okay; it will be okay."

It will be okay. His words reverberated; I wanted to believe him. "Well, what are we waiting for? Let's get going," I said with the most convincing smile I could muster.

He smiled in return. "Just watch me and do what I do," he called over his shoulder as he sped toward *Nini*.

Okay…watch and do what he does—simple enough. He motored forward, walked calmly to the bow, and pulled in the anchor line—a brief tug and the anchor popped neatly over the bow-roller. He returned to the cockpit and motored out of the anchorage, just like that.

"Hmm, I guess it's our turn, Kia." I motored forward, shifted to neutral, hopped out of the cockpit, jumped over the grab rail, and skipped to the bow. I braced myself against the bow rail and pulled, fast and hard—seventy feet of rope snaked out all over the foredeck. At last I reached the chain; it was much heavier, covered in sticky paste-like mud. I pulled hard; the anchor broke free, and the boat began a slow drift with the current. I secured the anchor, hopped up, dashed back to the cockpit, put the boat in forward, and looked around: couldn't turn left, too many boats. I turned the wheel hard to starboard. We were drifting to port, toward another boat.

"Not that way," Ed yelled.

"I know, I know!" I said aloud as I gave the boat throttle to tighten the turn, and in a few moments, we fell in behind *Nini*. The cell phone rang. We'd agreed earlier to use our cell phones, when possible, rather than the VHF to communicate.

"How's it going back there?" Ed asked.

"Not bad—not bad at all," I managed with a grin, my heart still racing, breath coming in gasps. I had survived weighing anchor.

"You're really going to have to show me that cute little dance thing again," he teased.

"What little dance thing?"

"That little hop-skip, dance-your-way-to-the-anchor-and-back thing you did," he said. "Quite entertaining."

"Ha-ha—very funny. Could you please speed it up a little? I'd like to get to the Bahamas sometime this year."

"Actually, no…I can't," he replied.

It didn't take long to realize that Ed's heavy ferro-cement boat with its twenty-seven-horsepower Yanmar engine just wasn't going to be able to motor as fast as mine. It was almost worth the loss of time to have something to tease him about. The nickname "Pokey" came to mind and stuck.

As the day progressed, I got a feel for how my boat moved: the fact that she turned easily to port, but you really had to crank the wheel to starboard. I learned how quickly she responded to the throttle, slowing down when I eased off. The miles slipped seamlessly by as we headed south down the Intercoastal, bound for West Palm and the Lake Worth Inlet. Dolphins swam in my wake; fellow cruisers waved as they passed, heading north for hurricane season. In a few short days we'd be staged in Lake Worth, ready to make the crossing to the Bahamas. I couldn't remember a time when I'd felt so alive. Ed had promised that within a few weeks of sailing I would become master of my vessel. I would feel its pulse, and my boat and I would work together as one. At the moment I was content to manage her enough to keep out of trouble.

"Commander, how's it going?" Ed called as he motored up a bit closer.

"Commander?"

"Ya, you look like you're driving a tank. Relax. You don't have to sit behind the wheel. Save the ten-and-two thing for your car."

"I am relaxed. I like sitting this way," I said indignantly, although I was envious of how at ease he seemed aboard his boat, moving around the cockpit, even leaving it from time to time. "And by the way, it's *Master and Commander* to you."

"Really...I think we'll have to discuss that later, but no matter," he said with a grin. Then he held up a chocolate bar—the kind I like—Cadbury fruit and nuts.

My stomach growled. Although Kia had a bowl of kibble and water, I hadn't thought to arrange snacks in the cockpit for myself, and now I was stuck. I couldn't let go of the wheel for more than a few seconds, so I couldn't go below to get anything. I would pass the day with nothing to eat or drink. Nothing to drink was actually a blessing since there was also nowhere to pee. Nonetheless, the more I thought about the hours that loomed ahead, the better that chocolate looked.

"Want some candy, little girl," Ed taunted.

"Sure, toss it over."

"Why don't you come over and get it?" He took a bite.

"Pull my boat up closer?"

"Yup," he answered.

"But I'll hit you."

"Don't," he said.

I turned the wheel slightly to port and the distance between us closed. We were about five feet apart.

"Closer…" he urged.

I turned a bit more, slowing down, and then there was three feet between us. "Throw it," I said.

He was standing on the deck, an arm's length away. "Come here and take it," he said, taking another bite.

I considered my alternatives…if I didn't do something quick, he'd probably eat the whole thing…I made sure the boat was holding its course, and with one hand still on the wheel, I crept crablike, sideways, over the cockpit combing and onto the deck. I glanced at Ed, and in one swift move, like an eagle after its prey, I swooped and snatched the chocolate from his hand. Then in the blink of an eye, I was back behind the wheel. I took a big bite. Chocolate had never tasted so good.

I can't believe you'd stoop so low, Kia's disapproving gaze seemed to say.

"Don't look at me like that," I said. "At least I don't go around sniffing for dead things to munch on." She looked away, snorted, then sighed deeply and closed her eyes.

We anchored as daylight was fading; we'd traveled only twenty-seven miles, but that was fine with me—the adventure had begun. I lagged behind a bit to watch Ed set his anchor. Then I motored in behind *Nini*, raced to the bow, and dropped the anchor. I waited for the boat to drift back with the current, waited for the telltale tug on the line that we'd discussed, to let me know my anchor had set; but it didn't drift back, and the line hung limp in the water. I looked toward Ed in confusion.

"You're still in forward," he called.

"What?"

"You forgot to put the boat in neutral. Pull up your anchor; try again," he yelled louder.

I heard him clearly this time. What an idiot I was. The whole day's success faded under the spotlight of my error. I pulled up the anchor, circled around…This time I remembered to put the boat in neutral. I dropped the anchor, waited a tense moment…it held. What a relief. Day one was officially over. One almost incident-free day down, many more to go; but for now I could rest. I was just recovering from the whole anchoring ordeal when the phone rang.

"Good job today," Ed said.

"What do you mean? I totally screwed up."

"You made it through the day with no damage to you or the boat. That makes it a good day. And...you won't make that mistake again."

"I guess...thanks," I said in an unconvinced tone.

"It's been a long day. Why don't you come over in a bit, and I'll make us some dinner. You don't want to miss my specialty."

"That would be nice, thanks." I was willing to risk the uncertainty of the dinghy ride for the safe warm feeling I got aboard Ed's boat. I spent a few moments getting everything ready for morning, then climbed into the evil dinghy.

"Come on, Kia girl." She jumped effortlessly into the small boat. I started the motor and untied the line. I took hold of the tiller and reminded myself, speaking aloud, "Left to go right, right to go left." Then, taking a deep breath, I shoved off. We were fast approaching *Nini*; Ed was on deck. Great...twenty feet and we made it. All I had to do now was turn in toward his boat...

"Where are you going? Was it something I said?" Ed called as we veered sharply away from the boat and out into the channel.

"This stupid thing won't go where I want it to," I yelled over the whir of the engine.

"The other way—no, no, the other way..."

"I know...hold on a minute." Finally, after a series of figure eights, I managed to get within crashing distance of *Nini* and successfully executed the "crash-bang, grab the side of the boat" docking maneuver.

"That was interesting," Ed said, taking the line from my hand and not quite managing or trying to suppress his smile.

"I hate this stupid dinghy—no, that's not true—I hate the motor. I'd rather row." I wanted to kick something; I looked at Ed.

"There, there, it's over now."

"Don't be condescending. Why can't you keep the dinghy and come and get us."

"We'll see. But right now let's take Miss Hound ashore; then you're in for a treat. I've made my Corned Beef and Egg Surprise."

I woke to a light breeze and sunny skies, feeling surprisingly refreshed.

"Good morning, Kia. How's my beautiful girl?" I set Kia's ramp against the ladder, and she bounded up to the cockpit.

"Are you ready to go pee-pee?" She wagged then trotted over toward where the dinghy was tied.

"No, no, pup, we're going pee-pee on deck." The wagging stopped abruptly. She watched suspiciously as I proceeded toward the bow and placed a three by three square of Astroturf on the deck.

"Come on; come here." She wouldn't budge. I took hold of her collar and led her over to the square.

"Good girl. Pee-pee, Kia. Go pee-pee."

She looked up at me for a second, sniffed the Astroturf, turned in a circle and turned a bit more, found the perfect spot, and laid down, right in the middle.

"No, Kia, this is not a bed. Go pee-pee." I tried again, leading her first off the mat, then urging her to pee. When for the fourth time she curled up in the center of the Astroturf, I gave up.

"Never mind, girl, we'll go ashore in a minute."

I brewed a pot of coffee and poured it into a thermos. I gathered some snacks and a few bottles of water and placed everything in the cockpit. Today would not be a repeat of yesterday, especially since we'd be traveling a much greater distance.

"Come on, Kia, let's go." We motored over to Ed's and used the crash-bang grab technique once again to bring the dinghy to a stop. Conveniently, the motor died when we hit the hull.

"Knock, knock, good morning," I called out.

"Is it?" Ed emerged looking exhausted. There were deep shadows darkening the normally white rings under his eyes.

"Ready for a potty run?"

"Hmm," he grumbled, and then climbed down into the dinghy.

Kia was more than ready. She jumped over the pontoon into the water, splashing us as she landed, and then swam ashore and dashed off into the shrubbery. She was back in minutes and bounded aboard as if this were something she'd been doing her entire life.

"She's really getting the hang of this. I think she likes the boating life."

"What about Kia's mother? Does she like the boating life?" Ed asked.

"I think so."

The anchor came up easily, even though the muscles in my arms burned from yesterday's exertions. Kia sat next to me and seemed to be enjoying the ride. She held her head high and looked around inquisitively. A dolphin surfaced, slicing through the water, then disappeared.

"Kia, look—a dolphin!" I pointed to port just as it surfaced again. She pranced over to the portside deck with her tail held straight and high and circling fast like a propeller. Two more dolphins appeared, dipping, diving, and leaping from the water.

"See, pup, this is what it's all about; this is why we're here." The sun was shining; there was a light breeze; I had a cockpit full of goodies; and for an instant, all was perfect in our little world.

Morning turned to afternoon, and as the miles slipped by, I began to feel little tinges of anxiety. Although everything was going well, there were still many things that made me nervous: bridges for one, especially when we had to wait for an opening. Sometimes from far away it was hard to tell which part of the bridge I was supposed to pass under. I stuck close to Ed, mimicking what he did. He'd approach from one side or another to compensate for wind or current. We were fast approaching the Memorial Bridge, and I turned my ship's radio to channel nine to listen as Ed hailed the bridge tender.

"Memorial Bridge, Memorial Bridge, this is southbound sailing vessel *Nini*," Ed called.

"This is the Memorial Bridge. What can I do for you, captain?"

"Memorial Bridge, I'd like to request an opening for two southbound sailboats."

"Southbound sailboats, this is the Memorial Bridge. We will be opening in just a minute; I have a northbound barge coming through before you. Please let the barge clear before you begin your approach."

I circled around to starboard in order to get out of the way of the oncoming barge and was about halfway through the turn when I felt a soft thud, a slight jerk, and then the boat stopped short. They say there are two types of boaters: those that have run aground and those that will. I put the boat in reverse, and to my relief it slid easily backwards, out of the muck. I looked over my shoulder to see if Ed had noticed and wondered if I was now one of those that had run aground. If a tree falls in the woods…

I didn't have long to ponder my grounding status, because as I changed gear to forward, nothing happened—and I mean nothing. The boat remained in reverse and was now moving at a pretty good clip—toward the barge. I grabbed the gear lever and pulled it back into neutral and then reverse; I tried forward again—nothing. If I didn't do something soon, I would most certainly motor right into the barge. I left the helm, reached down into the companionway, and pulled the engine stop, then ran to the bow and let loose anchor. The phone rang just as I'd secured the boat.

"What's going on?" Ed asked.

"My forward-reverse thingy isn't working. The boat's stuck in reverse."

"Can you come get me?" He asked. We'd decided to use my dinghy en route since I had dinghy davits. Ed's dinghy and outboard were stowed away.

Could I get him? If I had to swim over and carry him to the boat on my back, I'd have done it. We made it back to my boat just as the bridge tender called.

"Southbound sailboats, southbound sailboats, I can't hold traffic up forever. What's going on?"

Ed picked up the transmitter. "Sorry, we're having a bit of a problem with one of the boats. We'll call back once we're sorted out."

Ed dismantled the steering pedestal. One hour, one bolt, a cable tie, and some four-minute epoxy later, as we waved goodbye to the bridge tender, I wondered vaguely how many more near misses I was allowed. On the bright side, with today's potential disaster out of the way, I was free to relax and enjoy the sites along the waterway.

Dusk found us anchored in Mosquito Lagoon. We took Kia ashore, foregoing the Astroturf battle. The stress of yet another mechanical malfunction weighed heavy, and I was too exhausted to try and coax her to pee on deck.

"Why so quiet?" Ed asked as we motored slowly ashore in the dinghy.

"No reason. I feel like I could fall asleep right here in my seat. Do you mind? I think I'd like to skip dinner and just go to bed."

"No, that's fine. I'll probably read a bit and then do the same," Ed said.

Less than half an hour later, I was nestled cozy and comfortable in my bunk, looking forward to the only escape I had—sleep. Unbeknownst to me, I was destined to learn how Mosquito Lagoon got its name. When the assault began, I was in that twilight place—not awake, not yet asleep. At first I wasn't sure, perhaps my leg was just itchy, then my shoulder, and the back of my palm, and then I heard them—zZzzz zZzZzz—everywhere. I struck out, swatting blindly, only to hear the torturous zZzzz zZzZzz buzzing seconds later. They were fascinated with my ears. I swatted again, whacking myself in the side of the head. With my ear ringing, I turned on the light; at least that way I'd be able to see. I remained vigilant for a while and then I slept; and then I dreamed of waves crashing —a salty mist soothing my itchy irritated skin. I turned to the sea, welcoming its caress…then woke to a torrent of rain.

I was soaked; the bed was wet, and it was still only two-thirty in the morning. I closed the hatch, switched off the light, and surrendered myself to the steamy, sopping wet, now airless mess that was my bunk. There is a place beyond exhaustion and fear, and that place had become my home.

I sat on the port side sipping my coffee, every now and then adjusting the wheel; I was too tired to remain glued to the helm. I yawned, then stretched and wondered briefly what the day would bring. There was promise in the clearing skies. Mangroves and swaying palms graced the shoreline, replacing the homes of yesterday. Majestic herons stood frozen at the water's edge, and pelicans flew in formation overhead. The water rippled, and a sea turtle surfaced for an instant and then was gone. The palette was hewn in shades of blue and green, and the air was thick and alive.

Kia was seated just behind me, leaning against my back. She nudged me with her nose, and I turned to scratch the silky fur around her ears.

"You're tired, too, aren't you, girl?" She raised a paw, placed it on my arm, and looked into my eyes. Did she feel my uncertainty, the part of me that wondered what we were doing here? She nudged me once again as if to say, Alright, already, I just wanted you to pet me.

"We've got a long day ahead of us, pup, but at least it looks like we'll have good weather."

We motored lazily along, then entered an open expanse of water. Ed was about a half mile ahead when I saw his boat turn sharply—almost ninety degrees—to starboard, and he disappeared into the mangroves.

"What the heck?" I hadn't opened my charts, opting to follow his lead, but now I scrambled to get the book open to the appropriate page. A moment later, the mystery was solved: we'd reached the relatively narrow opening to the Haulover Canal. I motored forward, turned, and aimed for the seemingly miniscule gap.

Rock jetties flanked either side of the canal. Looking down its length toward the bridge I was filled with trepidation. There were several other sailboats ahead of us. What if we had to wait? How would I maneuver in a space that seemed barely wide enough for two boats? The phone rang.

"Come on. Hurry up. You have to get closer. They won't open till we're near the bridge."

The current was strong. Even at an idle I was moving forward at almost three knots. About halfway up the canal, I began to smell something strange, and the trees seemed to be closing in around me. I sniffed the air: burning rubber, that's what it was. I leaned over the side to make sure the exhaust was still pumping. Water was coming out, but the smell was definitely there. I popped my head down into the companionway and sniffed. Could the engine be on fire? With that thought in mind, I swung the boat around and headed back out toward the clearing. My phone rang again.

"What are you doing?" Ed sounded impatient.

"I think there's a fire on the boat. I have to get out of here."

"Are you sure?"

"No, but I smell something. I have to get out of here."

I looked back; Ed had turned and was following me. I fought the current up the canal, entered the lagoon, tossed out the anchor, and switched off the engine. I was still searching for the fire when Ed arrived. He threw me a line and climbed aboard, then descended to check the engine compartment; he looked and sniffed.

"Everything seems okay here," he said, then proceeded to the electrical panel. He opened the panel. "Everything seems okay here, too. What exactly did you smell?" he asked, climbing back up into the cockpit.

"It was a kind of burning rubber smell," I replied. I was coming down off the adrenaline high. Fatigue and stress had caught up. I felt like tempered glass about to shatter into a million pieces.

"Are you sure it wasn't the shrubbery?" he asked calmly.

"What?"

"I said, are you sure it wasn't the shrubbery?"

"The shrubbery," I repeated not comprehending.

"Ya. Didn't you notice the smell of the shrubbery? It was very strong in the canal." He stated matter-of-factly.

"No, I did not notice the smell of the shrubbery. What I did notice was the smell of burning rubber."

"I think it was the shrubbery," he repeated.

"Ed, I can't do this; I can't take anymore. I'm tired. I'm tired of waiting for the next disaster, of wondering what's going to break and when. My nerves are shot. I'm sorry, but maybe this was all a big mistake." If I kept talking, I knew I would end up in tears; I took a deep breath, swallowed, clenched and unclenched my jaw. "I want my life back. I want to sleep in a dry bed. I mean sleep, without bugs, without wondering where the boat will be when I wake up. I'm tired of stressing out. Every inch of my body is sore and bruised. I want to go back. You should go on without me. I'm going to stay here for a bit, then I'm heading back."

The silence was broken only by the gentle lapping of water against the hull. Ed looked at me and then at Kia, who wagged her tail tentatively. He looked up and down my boat, then at his, then toward the canal. His wheels were spinning, and I could see that he was about to say something.

"How about a cup of tea?" he asked. Even on the verge of hysteria, I had to smile. With Ed, when things got bad, it was tea time.

"Sure, tea would be nice."

We were quiet as I prepared tea, quiet as we sat and sipped. I lit a cigarette and inhaled deeply. Ed lit one. I studied the end of mine, flicking it frequently into the ceramic ashtray that he'd bought me in Saint Augustine. I studied the cracks in the ashtray, the spot where a chip of clay was missing; ceramics don't always hold up so well on a boat, and I'd already had to repair it twice. I looked up at Ed.

"Are you okay with my decision?"

"Are you?"

"Yes and no," I answered.

He nodded, waiting for me to continue.

"I'm so tired; you have no idea...But on the other hand, it's breaking my heart to give up before I've really even started. If I go home now, this will probably be it, and you've spent so much time helping me with the boat and teaching me. It's all going to go to waste." I couldn't tell him that it would break my heart to say goodbye.

"Then don't let it go to waste," he said. "If you go back now, you'll never know. There will never be a right time. I know people who have spent years getting ready, but they never untie the dock lines. Every time they're about to leave, they come up with something else that needs doing." He paused and drew a deep breath, then inspiration struck. "What if I tell you, you don't have a choice?"

I raised an eyebrow.

"Yes, really," he said reading my expression. "What if I tell you that you don't have a choice? You're coming with me whether you like it or not. If I have to tie you to the helm and tow your boat through that bridge, I will."

I laughed, and the mood lightened from the somber pre-tea gloom.

"Come on, you ungrateful wench. Poor me, after all I've done for you, you're just going to cast me off?"

"Ed, be serious for a minute." Even though I protested, I was happy that he wasn't letting me go that easily.

"I am serious," he said with an unreadable smile.

"Okay, tell me something: what else can go wrong?" I asked "We've fixed just about everything."

"Don't ask," he said.

"No, really, what else can go wrong?"

He looked at me, then out across the water and to his boat. He was quiet for a moment and then he took a deep breath and began softly.

"What else can go wrong? Everything…Everything you can see and everything you can't. That's why I gave you all those books to read. I don't want you to be afraid; I want you to be ready—to have a plan. You probably think I'm paranoid, pessimistic. I'm not; I'm a very positive person, but positive doesn't mean that things won't happen. Things will go wrong and most likely at the worst time, but knowing this I can make a plan."

I wanted to think he was exaggerating, but he wasn't. He was telling me to expect and be ready for anything. I'd been bobbing along hoping for the best, all the while fearing the worst; but with preparation, knowledge, and a plan for each situation, I'd be in control—or at least I'd feel like I was. Looking at it in that light, things didn't seem so bad anymore. Besides, I knew I couldn't go back; I wanted this too much—all of it: the adventure, the dream, the reality, the possibilities of what lay in store. And if stress, exhaustion, and a head of white hair to replace my mahogany tresses were the price, then so be it.

"Let's do it."

We motored back down into the canal, and again I felt it closing in on me. I could smell the burning rubber, but this time I knew and reminded myself that it was the rich smell of composting plants and soil. I took a deep breath and prayed.

"Please, God, help me do this. I have to do this. I can do this. I can do this. *I can do this…*" I repeated the mantra the entire length of the canal, then the bridge opened, and we passed calmly, uneventfully into a large body of water. I laughed with relief, motored confidently up to Ed's boat, dancing a happy dance at the helm.

"Come on, Pokey, speed it up a little," I teased. Ed watched wryly, no trace of amusement.

"Why so grouchy? We did it!"

"Yes *we* did, didn't we."

We anchored north of the Addison Bridge near Cape Canaveral. Still high on my success and feeling invincible, I climbed into the dinghy; Kia joined me. We were half way to Ed's when the outboard suddenly went from "vroom" to "sputter, sputter, putt putt…nothing." I pulled the cord and nothing. I pulled again, still nothing. We were downwind of *Nini* and drifting away. Luckily, I'd remembered the oars. It would have been even better if I knew how to use them. Was Ed watching? I looked over my shoulder and smiled sheepishly. Of course he was; he was always watching. I placed the oars in the oarlocks; I'd rowed both a kayak and a canoe in the past. How hard could this be? I dipped the oars into the water, preparing to propel the dinghy upriver toward Ed's boat; one oar skipped along the surface while the other dove deep and sent the dinghy into a tail-spin. I tried again with similar result. Apparently, rowing backwards with two oars required a completely different skill set. I was getting quite frustrated.

"Please, don't make me swim." I heard Ed's plaintive call.

"Please, don't make me swim," I mumbled and was sorely tempted to play the helpless damsel just to see him jump in. "It would serve him right." I smiled as I imagined him dripping wet, rowing us back to the boat.

Of course, pride won out; I climbed onto the nose of the boat, grabbed an oar, and began paddling kayak style, slowly upriver toward *Nini*. Ed was still shaking his head as he removed, cleaned, and replaced the spark plugs. Under his ministrations, the outboard sputtered and then sprang to life, and I found myself once again torn between the desire to strangle and to hug him.

"Ed, I was thinking…" I said as we motored along toward the shore.

"Ya, I know, saw the smoke."

"Why don't you keep the dinghy and come get me in the morning," I continued, ignoring his sarcasm.

"I can do that," he agreed, in a manner not quite his, and I couldn't help but be suspicious.

A gentle breeze wafted through the cockpit as we sat in companionable silence on my boat that evening and looked up at the night sky. The boat drifted slowly to the left, paused, and then drifted back.

"That constellation—what is it?" I asked pointing up into the dark.

"Orion—see the belt and sword."

I nodded. "He's my favorite. At night, I lie in my berth, and when I look up and see those stars, I know I'm okay; I know that the anchor is holding. Orion is keeping watch."

"That's cool. Just make sure you keep watch too."

"Ha-ha."

"I'm just saying," Ed said with a yawn. "I think I'm going to turn in. We need to get an early start."

"Okay, goodnight."

When Ed left, I ducked below, picked up my cell phone, and dialed my daughter's number. It had been several days since we last spoke.

"Hi, honey. How are you?"

"Pretty good. You?" Tanya asked.

"I'm *really* good actually. I'm starting to get the hang of all this boating stuff. By the time you get here...by the time we're ready to leave, I should have everything under control."

"That's awesome, Mom. *And*...how about Ed? How are things with him?"

"The same, I guess. Sometimes I think he's flirting with me and then I don't know. He's still definitely into his ex-girlfriend, though. I'm pretty sure of that. He talks about her all the time."

"Hmm..."

"What...what do you think? What should I do?"

"He's hard to figure out; I think you should talk to him."

"I can't do that."

"Why not?"

"Cause everything's good the way it is. I don't want to ruin things. Besides if he was interested in me, he'd do something, right? That's what guys do...don't they?"

"I don't know, Mom. Not everyone's the same. You asked me what you should do, and I told you. If you don't want to have a talk with him, don't. If you're happy with the way things are, then great."

"Whoa—someone's in a grouchy mood. It's okay honey, I'll figure it out myself…love you."

Tanya was so open and real she couldn't fathom why it was impossible for me to simply *have a talk* with someone—anyone. It was her solution to everything, and it worked for her.

After we hung up, I decided to tidy the boat a bit. I hadn't quite settled in yet, hadn't figured out where to put everything: my clothes were already in the hanging lockers and drawers, which have closures to keep them from flying open; my new unbreakable dishware sat in a protective cabinet in the galley; and there were storage lockers with shelves in which to keep foodstuffs, tools, charts, and books, but I had a small box full of miscellaneous mementoes that each needed a home.

Along the way I'd learned that Velcro came in very handy; whatever wasn't fastened down, tied, or bolted would at some point become a projectile. Even the sofa cushions were held in place with Velcro. So, armed with a roll of Velcro left by the previous owner, I set out on my mission.

At the moment I was most concerned with three special items: a small, carved Zuni fetish—a horse—that my mom had given me twenty years ago; a Saint Christopher medallion; and a polished, engraved stone. I picked up the stone, feeling its weight and smoothness. I traced the letters with my finger—SURRENDER. I closed my eyes, and thought back a couple of years to Tanya's senior year of high school…I'd been feeling restless. But Mom's illness, my business, and Tanya's pending graduation had made it difficult to contemplate any major life changes. That February, during Tanya's school break, we'd set off on a road trip from Boston to Florida. During the long hours over endless stretches of highway, punctuated by billboards and mile markers, the walls came down. Through laughter and tears, we drove and talked and sang. One night we stopped at a Cracker Barrel restaurant and browsed the gift shop while waiting for a table. On the checkout counter I saw a basket full of shiny rocks with words carved into them.

"Why don't we each choose a stone—our own personal quest?" I suggested. We began sorting through the rocks: LOVE, DARE, PROMISE, LIVE, REMEMBER, DANCE, GIVE.

"Mom, I found one." Tanya showed me her rock.

"IMAGINE," I read aloud.

My sweet, amazing girl was—and is—a realist, as deeply rooted as I am a feather in the wind. She's capable, loving, and strong. Imagination would give her wings—the rest she could do on her own.

"That's brilliant, honey," I said as I continued sifting through the stones: *HAPPINESS, DREAM, BELIEVE, JOY, FORGIVENESS.* "Oh, wait…Here it is…I found it—SURRENDER."

"Surrender…yeah, right. You're a control freak, Mom."

"I know. That's why I picked it."

I opened my eyes and was back in my boat. I closed my fingers around the stone and spoke the word aloud, "SURRENDER—I guess I'm still working on that one."

I reached for the Velcro and cut three small squares. I peeled away the protective liner and stuck one behind the rock, one on the back of the medallion, and one on the feet of the horse. I arranged them in the cockpit, on the wooden ledge above the companionway, where I'd be able to see them as I sailed. Saint Christopher, to protect us as we traveled; the horse, to guide us swift and true; and the stone, to remind me that control is an illusion—sometimes to surrender is to be free.

I climbed from my bunk the following morning with a revelation—this was my life. I had chosen to stick it out; I had mounted my talismans, and now I was committed. *Gypsy Spirit* was our home, mine and Kia's.

I heard the sound of a tail thumping happily and didn't have to look to know that Ed was on his way over. He pulled up, and Kia jumped nimbly into the dinghy. A moment later, Astroturf in hand, I plopped down across from him.

"Don't ask," I said in response to his raised eyebrow. The new plan was to get Kia to pee on the mat on land. Hopefully, recognizing her scent on the mat, she'd relieve herself on deck.

"This is almost as entertaining as the anchoring dance," Ed teased as I chased Kia in circles, trying to shove the mat under her each time she squatted to pee. Finally unable to hold it any longer, she gave me a scathing look, then waddled forward, peeing as she went.

"Thanks for your help."

"You're welcome. Hey, just a thought, but it's only twelve miles to Cocoa—why don't we head over now and spend the afternoon there? We'll have all day tomorrow there, too," Ed suggested.

The thought of having an entire day to kick back and relax was tempting. "Yeah, sounds good. Let's go."

Cocoa Village was a cruiser's dream, with the town center a short dinghy ride away, and everything we needed within walking distance. I was pleasantly surprised by the quaint buildings that housed galleries and cafés, gift shops and restaurants; there was a playhouse, a small grocer, and an amazing turn-of-the-century hardware store. I purchased a large monkey wrench and would finally be able to adjust my overly leaky stuffing box, which had been plaguing me since we started. We went to the post office and mailed Kia's application for a permit to enter the Bahamas.

We spent the morning meandering through the village. I was in my element and longed to find a little café and kick back for a while, but I could see that Ed was getting antsy.

"What's the matter, don't you like it here?" I asked

"It's great, but we've seen it now...Why don't we get back to the boats. If we leave soon, we could reach Melbourne and still have a couple hours of daylight."

"You said we could spend the whole day."

"I know, but is there anything else you need to do?"

"No, not really."

"I know you want to explore and have fun, but our goal is to get to the Bahamas. We're already into hurricane season, and once the storms start, we'll be heading home. Wouldn't you rather have more time in the islands?"

Several incident-free days bolstered my confidence, and if all went well, we'd anchor in Lake Worth by nightfall. Thankfully, going through bridges wasn't such a harrowing undertaking anymore. In this final leg, there was a bridge every mile or so. At long last we reached the PGA Bridge, the final one on our journey to the Lake Worth Inlet. As luck would have it, the bridge was under construction. Openings were limited, and half of the bridge remained closed during the opening. A barge parked in the channel created even more of an obstruction. I motored in behind Ed and shifted to neutral, waiting for the great arm of the bridge to rise. Suddenly the engine surged; an alarm sounded on the console; there was a lot of grey smoke, and then the engine died. *Gypsy Spirit* began drifting toward *Nini* and the barge. I reached down into the companionway and jammed my finger into the ignition button; my heartbeat seemed to match the rhythm of the engine as it struggled to life. It misfired then started with a vroom and a blast of white smoke. I breathed a sigh of relief. The engine didn't sound quite right, but it got me through the bridge and over to Little Lake Worth. I was setting the anchor when the engine died once again, and this time it would not start.

The week passed in a frantic blur of activity. Friday arrived and with it the knowledge that I would not be leaving for the Bahamas with Ed. We'd spent days trying everything to get the engine running. Ed started by looking into the most obvious culprits. He bled the fuel system; we had the fuel injectors rebuilt and bled the system again. We purchased a new alternator (unrelated, but needed), tuned the cylinders, and bled the fuel system countless more times. We tried to find a diesel mechanic but got only answering machines. As the days passed, we ran out of options. Ed's visa would expire very soon; he had no choice but to leave.

"I think you should call TowBoat US and arrange to be towed to a marina," he said.

"Wow, next you'll be suggesting tea," I said in a weak attempt at humor.

"It's not that I want to leave—I have to leave. I have to leave tomorrow, actually," he said suddenly.

"I know. It's okay. We both knew this could happen, and it's been great—really it has. Just the trip down the waterway was amazing," I said bravely. Now was not the time to wonder what the heck I was going to do once the engine was fixed. Motoring back to Saint Augustine, alone, tail between my legs, was not my idea of the perfect ending.

"It's not over," he said, reading my mind.

"Yes, it is."

"No, this is a temporary hiccup. You'll get your engine fixed and join me."

I stared in disbelief. And he accused me of smoking the funny stuff? Did he really think I was going to motor out the inlet—*alone*; cross the Gulf Stream—*alone*; and then find him somewhere in the Bahamas? He apparently had more faith in me than I did in myself. My thoughts were interrupted by the phone.

"Hello," I answered. "Yes, I called. Thanks for getting back to me. It's a sailboat: fifty-horsepower Perkins...Uh-huh...a 4-108...No, nothing. It turns over but won't start. I think the battery's beginning to lose juice too...I'm traveling with a friend but he has to leave tomorrow." I looked over at Ed and smiled hopefully.

"I was hoping there was something that could be done today...I see. No, tomorrow morning will be great, thank you...I'm anchored in Little Lake Worth. I can pick you up from the dinghy landing if that works for you...Okay, thanks... Yes, see you tomorrow."

"The mechanic's going to meet us here at nine o'clock in the morning," I said.

"Good—very good. Give me your GPS. I'm going to program in some waypoints. Let's do this. If he gets the boat running and you can leave by noon, plot a course just south of east and head over. At your speed you'll catch up with me before I reach the bank. If I get there before you, I'll wait."

My heart sunk. I had hoped he'd stay now that a mechanic was on the way. "What if we can't get the engine running? How will you know? How long will you wait on the bank?"

"Through the night," he said. "If you're not there by morning, I'll head on."

"How do I find you?"

"I'll show you. See…here's Memory Rock," he said, pointing to a waypoint on my computer chart. "I've put this point in your GPS. The Gulf Stream current flows north, about three knots, at the strongest point. By keeping your heading south of east, you'll account for drift." At my look of confusion, he added, "Okay…look, I'm adding a couple more points—just in case. See here…Little Bahamas Bank, and here's Mantanilla Shoal. If you miss Memory Rock, you still have these two points."

What exactly was a *waypoint*? We hadn't covered them in our previous discussions; it had been boat-handling, sail trim, anchoring, and foul-weather tactics. "What will I see when I get there—to the waypoint I mean?"

"Nothing—just water. A waypoint is an arbitrary navigational point, but actually there is a beacon at Memory Rock."

"Hmm…I see," I said, not seeing at all. "Cool, yeah, that could work."

"Come on—don't worry. Let's go for a swim, then we'll have lunch, and I'll explain some more," Ed said.

I didn't know how to say goodbye, how to thank him for all he'd done. I wanted to give him a hug, but he was distant, and I hesitated, feeling awkward.

"What time are you leaving?" I asked.

"I'd like to be underway about half past five, make it to the inlet by six, and catch slack tide."

"Okay, well, stay safe and take care." It was all I could manage before climbing off *Nini*'s stern and into my dinghy.

"I will, and don't worry. Take care of the engine, and we'll work out the rest."

I didn't have the heart to tell him that I would not be making that crossing; I smiled, waved goodbye, and motored away. Then, feeling very much alone, I climbed into my berth, closed my eyes to the world, and slept—long and deep.

Daylight flooded the cabin; I blinked several times in the bright morning light and rubbed my eyes, then stumbled groggily into the main salon. I lifted Kia's ramp into place.

"Up-up, girl. Come on, up-up." Kia leapt nimbly from the portside settee onto the ramp and up to the cockpit. I followed her up and looked out over the water. Ed was gone...not even a ripple disturbed the surface where *Nini* had been. Kia stuck her head between the lifelines; she looked and sniffed; she tilted her head this way and that, listening for the familiar sound of the dinghy motor.

"He's gone, pup. He had to go," I said, petting her. "We'll be okay; don't you worry."

Maybe if I closed my eyes for just a second, then opened them, he'd still be there. We'd go ashore; we'd sit and talk over coffee. He'd tell me about the islands: how clear the water, how beautiful the fish; he'd tell me once again how we'd anchor by a deserted island and spend the day combing for shells. I closed my eyes, squeezed them tight, then opened slowly and looked out across the empty expanse of water. Shading my eyes with my hand, I turned toward the inlet. "Goodbye, Ed. Smooth sailing."

The Anti-Ed

Mid-October 2006

Oasis Boatyard
Saint Augustine, Florida

A month passed, and I was still grinding; the delamination on the impacted side seemed to go on forever. I'd ground away the gel-coat and much of the glass from the hole, midship all the way to the stern. I was trying not to get discouraged but it wasn't easy—seemed my motivation had burned out with the motor of my first grinder.

I moved into the Seaway Motel; the dust inside the boat was getting unbearable, and I was afraid for Kia's health and mine. While it was nice to sleep in a clean bed and be able to leave work at the end of the day, my new living arrangement created a complication. I met someone; actually, I'd met him the previous month at the motel when I'd first arrived in Saint Augustine, but now that I lived there we began spending time together, taking walks at night on the beach with Kia. His name was Ben, and he was the anti-Ed—exuberant and unrestrained. He looked and acted much younger than his forty years, and at first I found this refreshing. I enjoyed the easygoing friendship, but I didn't want to hurt or mislead him. I told him about Ed, how we were going to finish the boat and go sailing. I suggested that it would be best if we limited our time together.

Ben argued, "Ed will be here soon and then you'll be gone; don't take my fun away now. Stop worrying—relax. We're just friends."

But I was worried—very worried. As much as I enjoyed the companionship, I realized that along the way we'd crossed the "just friends" line into something else—though what, I wasn't sure. To complicate matters further, I soon realized that he had a drinking problem, and I suspected drugs as well. But when he was with me, he didn't drink as much, and I hoped I could at least help him get his life back on track.

I wished Ed were around; things would have been so much simpler. I had been both surprised and relieved when he first offered to come and help, especially since he'd been so against the idea of repairing the boat. Three months, I kept reminding myself; he'd be here in three months; we'd finish the boat and then we'd go sailing.

Ed and Kia…chillin aboard Gypsy Spirit

You Can Check In Anytime You Like...

July 2005

Riviera Beach Municipal Marina
West Palm Beach, Florida

What an odd predicament—I needed a mechanic, but this just seemed wrong. I was about to meet a strange man on the side of the road and ferry him back to my boat... My anxiety grew as I tied off the dinghy and made my way up an embankment toward the road; this went against every rule of caution I'd learned growing up.

"Christine?" asked the man as he stepped out from the white van.

"Yes...Jimmy?" He nodded, and I extended a hand. "I really appreciate you coming out on a Saturday and on such short notice."

"No problem. You're lucky you're a woman."

"Really, why?"

"A woman traveling alone on a sailboat…my curiosity was piqued." At my look of surprise he added, "It's not every day you hear about a woman single-handing a boat."

"That's true, but I'm not really alone. Like I mentioned, my boyfriend had to clear out ahead of me…because of his visa. He's waiting for me…on the bank. I need to make it out the inlet by noon."

"We'll see about that…hopefully it's nothing too serious," he said, then strode, tools in hand, down the slope toward the dinghy.

"Coming?" he asked.

I reminded myself that he was a known entity—known, that is, by the guy who fixed my fuel injectors—and he came highly recommended. I followed him down the slope, and we climbed into the dinghy.

"So, tell me, what kind of guy leaves his girl stranded?"

"I'm not stranded. Besides, he didn't have a choice," I said in a tone that suggested we end the discussion.

"How long have you been seeing this guy?"

"Look, I really don't want to discuss it."

"Whoa—sorry. I was just curious. Touchy subject, eh?"

I turned my attention to the outboard, and a moment later we arrived at the boat. Kia pranced over to greet us.

"Good girl," I said, petting her. "Have you been taking care of the boat, my big ferocious girl?" As if on cue, Kia looked down at Jimmy and growled. I was amazed; somehow she knew, sensed that I was nervous.

"By the way," I said, gesturing toward Kia, "she's very protective, so be really careful. You don't want to make her nervous—no sudden moves, things like that." I relaxed at his look of uncertainty.

"She bite?" he asked.

"Huh? No. I don't think so anyway."

Kia sniffed his leg while he stood nervously still. I had to stifle a laugh, imagining the worst she might do was goose him.

"The engine?"

"This way." I climbed down ahead of him and opened all four engine access panels, then pushed the start button for him to hear.

"Sounds like it's air-locked; you're not getting any fuel. Have you bled the system?" he asked.

"At least ten times."

"These Perkins can be tricky. You have to bleed them in two places, then at all four injectors and in sequence."

Hmm...two places, four injectors and in sequence—maybe there was hope. I followed, watching what he did, and felt more comfortable now that his attention was on the engine.

"So, tell me more about your boyfriend," he said, just as I was beginning to get comfortable.

"Nothing to tell actually. What about you?" I asked, noticing his wedding ring.

"*What* about me?"

I was startled by the sharpness of his response. "Nothing."

He sighed. "Sorry about that. Yeah, married...twelve years...just found out she's cheating on me. We have two kids."

Now I understood...the odd behavior, the borderline unhinged look. "I'm sorry to hear that."

"Yeah, well, it sucks. I don't know what to do. We've got kids." He paused. "Sometimes I get so mad. What the f**k does she want anyway? Let her get out there and try to make a living. You know what I'm saying…let her get off her lazy ass and see what it's like! That'll teach her!" He was almost shouting; his face was red, and his eyes were bright.

"Well, hopefully everything works out for the best," I said as pleasantly as possible. At his scowl, I added, "For the children's sake."

"You know what...I'm going to try ether."

"*What?*"

"*Ether*," he repeated loudly, as though I were deaf. "I'm going to try spraying ether into the air intake. That should get the engine started."

Oh. He was talking about the engine. I breathed a sigh of relief.

One quick blast and the engine started; the sound was music to my ears—slightly out of tune, but music nonetheless.

"Don't get too excited. It's not running right. I think you have a couple of bad cylinders."

"What does that mean?" I asked.

"It means you're not going anywhere."

"For how long?"

"It will be at least Tuesday before I can start working on it, and then depending on what I find…It would be easier if you were in a marina."

"Yeah, I was kind of planning on that."

"*Gypsy Spirit?*" the young man driving the red-striped TowBoat US pontoon boat asked.

"Hi, that was quick."

"A boat grounded nearby; I was just finishing up with them when your call came. You're lucky—holiday weekend and all. Where to?"

"Riviera Beach Municipal Marina...I hope. I've been calling them since yesterday, but no one picks up."

"I'm not surprised. I'll try them on the VHF; let's get you in the harness and start heading that way. It's going to rain in a bit," he said, looking in the direction of the thunderheads that I hadn't noticed till that moment. "Hopefully we'll make it there before the squall. It's a madhouse by the marina—boats everywhere. I'm going to tow you from my stern till we get past the Blue Heron Bridge. Once we're in the basin, I'll bring you into the marina on a hip tow."

"What should I do?" I asked.

"Just stay at the helm and steer."

Kia sat by my side, ears flapping in the strong breeze, while gigantic cauliflower-like thunderheads formed overhead. Beyond the bridge, boats were anchored everywhere; it would be chaos if the squall hit while we were weaving through that maze. The first wild rush of wind hit when we were still about a mile from the bridge, and tossed my boat on its side like a plastic tub toy.

"You okay back there?" the driver called over the VHF.

"Yes, we're fine," I answered.

"This'll be over pretty quick. It's good that it happened here. I'm going to slow down—let the storm pass."

As quickly as it came, the wind subsided, replaced by a torrent of rain through which Kia glared at me accusingly.

"Don't look at me like that. I didn't plan this."

She stood, stared me in the eye and then...she shook—vigorously.

"Thanks." I could swear she was grinning. "You know, maybe today would be a good time for that *bath*!" Ears dropped, she sat with a harrumph.

The sun returned, erasing all signs of the deluge. We passed under the bridge and entered a world in sharp contrast to the meandering channels and tranquil anchorages we'd experienced on our trip south. Ahead of us, Peanut Island formed a manmade buffer between the Intercoastal and the inlet. Strains of laughter and music overpowered the hum of the engine. Colorful campsites and small boats lined the shore of the island. Powerboats, sailboats, dinghies, and jet skis filled almost every inch of open water. Swimmers splashed in the shallows between boats, as jet skis idled by. It was a gigantic watery playground; the only clear area was the narrow stretch of waterway indicated by the red and green markers. As we reached the marina entrance, the driver slowed and then stopped. He brought his boat alongside mine and attached a harness for the hip tow, which would bring us in side by side.

"Were you able to get through to the marina?" I asked

"No, but it's no surprise. Don't worry—we'll find you a slip," he assured me.

The same party atmosphere pervaded the marina: people crowded the docks; music blared from the Tiki bar; and a band played in the park. It was overwhelming, and I missed the quiet of the last anchorage. The chaos made me feel even more alone. We turned and entered a labyrinth of channels. I saw two men on the outermost dock; they were watching our approach, and from a distance, the tall one reminded me of Ed. They laughed and waved and seemed to find it funny that I was being towed in.

"Hey, hello," I yelled, waving back. "I'm trying to get hold of the marina, but there's no answer."

"What?" the one that looked like Ed called back.

"I need a slip. Do you guys have any idea where I could go?" I yelled louder.

"Yes, yes, this way," said the smaller man pointing.

"Did you hear? He's going to show us where to go," I called to the driver.

"Yeah, I heard," he said, throttling down.

We followed the fairway into the marina and turned right where our guide gestured. The driver eased my boat, bow first into a slip near the end of the channel.

"Hi there, my name's Clive," said the man who'd guided us in.

"I'm Christine. Thanks for your help."

"Not a worry. You'll need a spring line. And be careful—the docks are fixed. Keep an eye on the lines till you get them set right," Clive said.

"Yeah, I will. Thanks again. By the way, where is your accent from?"

"South Africa," he said.

"Oh my god—what a coincidence—I'm traveling with a guy from South Africa."

"Oh, right—where's he hiding then?"

"What?" I asked confused.

"We figured you had some bloke aboard, hiding below, embarrassed about being towed in. That's why we were laughing."

"No, no," I laughed, "he has his own boat. He had to clear out. He's on his way to the Bahamas. As soon as my engine's fixed, I'm going to join him. It's so odd, though, meeting another South African."

"You're going to meet a few more. The guy you saw on the dock with me, Vaughan, he's South African. And then there's Pirate Pete and Lucky Mike," Clive said.

I laughed. "I can't wait." Suddenly it didn't seem so bad here after all; I had happened upon a virtual stockpile of handsome South African men.

"Great, well then, I'll leave you now. Catch you later?"

"Yeah, thanks again, Clive. Bye." I watched him disappear. "C'mon, pup, let's go for a walk and check this place out."

Kia tugged at the leash; she wanted to go back to the boat. She didn't like the noise and chaos of the marina; truth be told, neither did I. Sunset found me sitting in the cockpit, feeling sorry for myself, and thinking about Ed. Had he waited for us on the bank? Was he anchored in some idyllic spot? Was he thinking about me? It was hard to believe that just days ago we were making plans for all the wonderful things we would do in the Bahamas, and now here I was—alone.

Ed called Monday afternoon, just two days after he sailed off.

"You made it."

"Ya, I'm in Spanish Cay. Cleared in just now."

"You sound exhausted."

"Been going nonstop. What's up with the engine?" He asked.

"It's a holiday today—Fourth of July. The mechanic's coming tomorrow. I'm at a marina."

"Good. Listen...I've been thinking. I'm two days from the airport. I could leave my boat here, fly to West Palm and then we'll sail back together on your boat. What do you think?"

"I think that would be great...But what about the engine? The mechanic seems to think it might not be that simple."

"Ya, well...I'll wait till you give me the word. As soon as it's fixed, I'll fly back. Just get it done. Okay?"

"Okay, I will."

"I'll give you a call on Wednesday," he said.

I was on cloud nine; my story would have a happy ending, and our adventure would continue. The world turned shades brighter, and nothing could bring me down: not the engine situation, not my less-than-desirable new home port, not even the creepy mechanic who had now completely dismantled the engine. That's right—by one o'clock in the afternoon, the cabin floor was a jigsaw puzzle of engine parts, and still no solution. The new plan consisted of the mechanic taking all the miscellaneous bits to his shop for inspection.

"When are you going to put it back together?" I asked.

"It'll be at least a week before I can get started. I've got a big job before yours."

"A week! I wish you'd told me that before you took everything apart."

He ignored me and continued, "I have an idea…if you're willing. I'll come get you in the morning; bring you to the shop; tell you what to do; and you do it. You'll save time and money."

The idea seemed really strange—more than strange, it seemed bizarre. But I was desperate.

I hesitated for a moment. "Okay, what time?" I asked.

"I'll be here at 7:00 a.m. sharp."

After spending three days at Jimmy's shop, accompanying him to breakfast and lunch, and listening to his marital woes—sprinkled with something that might have been an attempt at flirtation—and after getting virtually nowhere in regard to the engine, I'd had enough.

"See you in the morning," he said as I climbed out of his van.

"I don't think so."

"Oh, okay…you busy tomorrow? I'll just pick you up on Monday then," he said.

"No, not Monday either. This is not working out for me. Why don't you just reassemble the engine and bill me for your time," I said.

"That's fine…just don't expect to be going anywhere for a while. Like I said, I've got a big job ahead of yours."

Great—he was holding my engine hostage. I had never felt so helpless. It had been okay when Ed was here, but he wasn't here now. To make matters worse, he hadn't called on Wednesday, and I was growing ever more concerned for his safety. There had already been two hurricanes, and one of them had crossed the Bahamas just a day ago.

That evening, after several long hours of internal debate, and knowing Ed would be furious, I broke down and contacted BASRA (Bahamas Air and Sea Rescue Association). I described *Nini* and Ed, and gave them the details of his passage. At that point, I no longer cared if he got angry; I had to do something, and this call would either save his life or embarrass him to death.

I squinted, bleary-eyed, at the phone. The insistent ringing had awoken me from a particularly unpleasant dream about being caught in a storm at sea. But at the sight of the Bahamian area code, I was instantly awake, certain that I was about to hear that they'd found him.

"Hello?" I answered breathlessly.

"Well, hello there."

"Ed? It's you. You're okay. They found you!" I said relieved.

"Yes, it's me. Why wouldn't I be okay? And who found me?"

"Oh…umm…nothing. I mean—it's you, yea…that's great. I just woke up; sorry if I sound confused. So anyway…" I said, shaking my head to clear the cobwebs. "How are you? I was so worried."

"Not worried enough to do something stupid I hope," Ed said.

"Huh?"

"Hopefully you weren't considering calling BASRA, especially after our discussion."

"Not considering it—no," I assured him.

"Good," Ed said.

"Anyway, so what happened?" I asked.

"Ya, I'm only now able to call. There was a hurricane. Did you hear?"

"Yes, that's why I was so worried."

"Ya, well, all good now. What's up with the engine?"

I blurted out the story and finished with, "So that's where we are now…he has the engine, and I don't know when I'll get it back."

"Okay, here's what you need to do. Call the mechanic; tell him your boyfriend is back, and he's really upset. He wants to come get the engine," Ed said.

"My boyfriend…who's my boyfriend?" I asked.

"That's not the point. Ask someone, anyone…ask Clive, I'm sure he won't mind."

Clive arrived while I was in the process of cancelling the BASRA search for Ed.

"Someone's in trouble," Clive sang. "I heard you talking to BASRA," he continued as he plopped onto the stool next to me. "Coffee, please," he called to the waitress.

"I cancelled the search before they found him, so he doesn't know. How weird is that, though. He called the very morning after I initiated the search."

"See, if you had listened to me…ah, well…so when does he get back?" Clive asked.

"As soon as the engine's fixed, then we'll sail back together to the Bahamas."

Clive was suddenly quiet.

"What's the matter?" I asked.

"Nothing, don't worry about it," he said. Then, at my look of dismay, he added, "More importantly, what shall we have for breakfast, and what do I get for keeping my silence about this whole rescue mission thing?"

"Very funny," I said. "But seriously, what's wrong?"

"You want to know…I'll tell you. I am sitting here wondering what kind of bloke leaves his girl stranded. What does he mean…fix the engine and then I'll come fetch you…I'm sorry but I just don't like it."

I felt really bad about my deception. Telling everyone that Ed was my boyfriend had seemed harmless at the time. I hadn't thought of the implications for him. It was time to set things straight.

"Listen, I haven't been completely honest."

"Aha—I knew you were a spy. Come now, admit it," Clive said.

I laughed. "It's about Ed."

"Ed…Ed…Ed…it's always about Ed," Clive said.

"No. Listen. Ed isn't really my boyfriend. I thought it would be better if people thought I had a boyfriend, but all I accomplished was to make him seem like some kind of deadbeat, which he isn't. He's helped me so much—you have no idea."

"Why are you telling me now?" Clive asked.

"Because you guys are all thinking the worst of him."

"Okay, so Ed's not your boyfriend. He's a great guy who helped you out. Now what?" Clive asked.

"I get my engine fixed, and he flies back."

"And then you tell him you're crazy about him, and the two of you sail off into the sunset and live happily ever after?"

"Whoa, where did that come from?" I asked.

"I don't know. I thought we were coming clean, telling the truth," Clive said.

"Ed and I are friends. That's the truth. By the way, before I forget, I have a really big favor to ask."

Twenty-four hours and one car rental later, Clive and I returned from Jupiter with my engine in the trunk.

"How weird was that?" I asked.

Clive shrugged.

"I mean, I don't get it."

"Guess he didn't want to meet your infamous boyfriend."

"I know, but...I can't believe he wasn't even there. Then he answers my call and says he left the key in the bathroom and we should let ourselves in and put the key back when we're done. What's up with that? We could have emptied his entire shop. What if I hadn't left him a check?"

"I don't think he was worried about the check."

We spent the next week rebuilding the engine, piece by piece, relying on my memory, notes, and Clive's mechanical knowledge. Putting the engine back together was one thing; getting it to run was completely another; and I was back to the drawing board.

No matter that I maintained a positive outlook, one thing was certain, the engine would not start, and home was now this poverty-ravished neighborhood where prostitutes as young as twelve languished steps from multimillion-dollar McMansions. Derelict boats littered the water around Peanut Island. Crackheads and runaways lived on the boats and in the park by the beach. I watched babies play barefoot at the water's edge while daddy lit up nearby. This was most certainly a place of lost hope, a place where dreams came to die and desperation hung in the air like a cloying perfume. Story after story, the tales were similar: came for a few days; still here after a few years; while boats moldered in slips, and captains drank themselves into oblivion at the Tiki bar.* Not my story; I'd be gone in a week, two at most. I was sure of it, even though discordant strains of "Hotel California" reminded me that *I could check in any time I liked, but I could never leave*. Problem was, everyone was a diesel mechanic, and the ones that I should have work on my engine didn't want to touch it. I was running out of options and had never felt so helpless.

The acceptance phase followed and then my days and weeks fell into a pattern. Go to the park in the morning; it was cool and quiet in the early hours of the day. If Kia and I were lucky, we'd see Walter and his dog, Magic, before they left for work. Kia and Magic would chase each other while I tried to cajole Walter into taking a look at the engine. Walter was the first mechanic recommended to me by the guy who rebuilt my injectors, even before Jimmy. He was a kind older man, but he had absolutely no interest in getting involved with my engine.

---

*As of my 2010 visit, Riviera Beach Municipal Marina had undergone dramatic renovations. Management was very much present. The bathrooms and laundry facilities were new. Many of the derelict vessels surrounding Peanut Island had been removed and the area in general seemed to be to experiencing economic recovery.

"I'm too old to be mucking around in the bilge of a sailboat," he said when I asked. He was, however, interested in the status and so I'd bring him up to date during our morning park meetings. I told him of the progress that Clive and I had made, but that the engine stubbornly still did not start. I told him I was looking into a new—or perhaps a rebuilt—engine. I told him about the latest diesel mechanic who'd visited.

Then it was off to the Tiki bar for coffee with Clive and Gary and Diesel Bob and whoever else happened to be there. Plot and scheme and discuss the latest strategy for solving the engine dilemma. Long walks with Kia and swimming by Peanut Island filled in the afternoon. I spent my evenings at Vaughan and Cindy's boat. Cindy had invited me for dinner the first night, and soon I became a regular at their place; I made friends and became part of the community. I met Barefoot and Carol, Pirate Pete and Lucky Mike. Lucky Mike was from South Africa, and he had written a book called *Dancing on Raindrops*. He was an adrenaline junkie: skydiver, BASE-jumper, sea captain, and adventurer. I was fascinated with his stories, and Lucky encouraged me to give skydiving a shot even though flying was the greatest fear of my life. Eventually, I agreed, thinking perhaps if I faced that fear, all others would pale in comparison; it would most certainly give meaning to my time here in West Palm. Like I said before, sometimes you just have to breathe deep and take a leap of faith. And that's what I did…

Pirate Pete, also from South Africa, was another story, and we regarded each other from a distance for a number of weeks. I respected him as a sailor and was somewhat in awe; I marveled at the fact that this giant of a man, who stood about six foot five inches tall, had sailed around the world one and a half times on a twenty-six-foot sailboat without an engine. He was soft spoken and had a little dog, a Jack Russell terrier named Skip. Skippy was as standoffish toward Kia as Pete was with me. Although he was very much a part of the group and definitely a close friend of Vaughan's, Pete lived out on the hook and kept to himself more than the others. He preferred the tranquility of the anchorage, even with its hardships, to the chaos of the marina.

In August, Tanya and her boyfriend arrived as planned. I was thrilled to see my daughter, but the knowledge that I had let her down weighed heavy. This was to be the start of our adventure, and we were no closer now than we had been in Saint Augustine. School would be starting up in just a few weeks, and Tanya wouldn't be there. She was taking the semester off; I'd convinced her that the experience she would gain sailing would be well-worth the time lost; and now instead of a sailing adventure, our days were spent in equal parts divided between beach, boat, and Tiki bar—definitely not what I had in mind.

About a week or so after Tanya's arrival, Ed returned—unexpectedly. He sailed in on the early morning tide, midway through August and hurricane season. He slipped into the marina and back into my life as quietly as he'd left. We barely skipped a beat.

No sooner had Ed arrived, Hurricane Katrina began forming over the Bahamas. We watched the news with trepidation, and when it became clear that we were directly in Katrina's path, we began gathering food, emergency supplies, and fresh drinking water. For two days, a steady stream of provision-laden carts coursed the docks. We doubled and tripled-up on dock lines, weaving the boats safely within polyester webs. I took down the dodger and Bimini and secured anything that could be blown or tossed from deck. Darkness fell on August 25, 2005—the eve of Katrina. Tanya sat perched in the cockpit, camera in hand, nervous but excited, while her boyfriend wore a decided look of apprehension; he'd gotten seasick recently and didn't relish the thought of sleeping on a heaving, rolling boat. We didn't quite know what to expect, but it was already evident that this storm would not meet its forecasted potential, and no evacuations had been ordered. Over the next few hours, the wind picked up, blowing a steady thirty-five knots with gusts to seventy; the boat rocked and rolled and tugged on its lines, but as luck would have it, the peak of the storm arrived with low tide, and we escaped the storm surge as well.

Katrina made landfall near West Palm as a moderate Category 1 hurricane, sparing us the devastation it would bring to the Gulf coast from Florida to Texas, during its second landfall as a Category 3. It would become one of the five deadliest hurricanes in U.S. history; almost two thousand people would lose their lives.

Tanya stayed with me for another few weeks, but by then it was quite clear that the boat would not be ready in time to go cruising. And so with a heavy heart, I drove her to the airport for her return trip to Massachusetts. Later that evening, Ed and I were sitting alone on my boat. I was going over different engine scenarios in my head...perhaps I could find a diesel mechanic in Saint Augustine and get him to come down to West Palm.

"How about we give it another shot?" Ed broke the silence.

"What...give what another shot?"

"Cruising the islands. We get that engine fixed and go sailing—maybe go to the Dominican Republic. I don't have to be back in South Africa until June. That would give us about ten months."

Ten months…I tried to remain calm, but it was hard; maybe Tanya would be able to join us at some point; not as a long a trip, but better than nothing. And *so* much could happen in ten months, but—and that was a big *but*—the engine.

"And the engine?"

"I have an idea about that. Walter said he didn't want to muck around inside your boat. What if we brought the engine to him?"

"But that's impossible—we'd have to take the boat apart."

"I don't think so."

"A lot of people looked; they said there was no way to get it out."

"Yes, that's right—they looked. There's a difference, you know, between looking and seeing."

"Okay, never mind that for a minute. Let's say you can get it out and Walter fixes it—you know that means I'll be following you around for another ten months," I teased.

"Following me? I thought I was following you," he said.

"You're following me?"

"Duh, I wouldn't be here right now if it weren't for you," he offered logically.

"Okay, well, that means you'll be following me around for the next year. I guess I'm okay with that."

"I'm sure you are," he said.

"You are *so* damn arrogant."

Walter agreed to rebuild my engine. If we could get it to his shop, he would do the work; and thank goodness for that, because it was no longer a matter of just getting it started. Ed and I had tried starter fluid, and the engine had sputtered to life, but then it dropped a connecting rod and burst the block. I'm not sure if that had to do with how I reassembled the engine or something that happened at the mechanic's shop. Anyway, once again the engine was dismantled; Ed stripped it down as much as possible, then rigged a pulley system through the opening ports and walked the engine sideways out of the compartment. He used the boom vang to bring the engine up the companionway and out onto the dock.

Just a day after the engine went to Walter's shop, October spawned yet another hurricane—Category 5 Wilma, the strongest tropical cyclone ever recorded in the Atlantic basin. And this time we did not escape. Again the harried race to prepare, but it was different somehow: quieter, busier. Perhaps we knew—sensed the angry churning energy raging toward us. Again the steady stream of dock carts, this time they carried water rather than beer, and candles in place of chips and salsa. By the time it reached land on the west coast of Florida, the storm had weakened to a Category 2, and the marina exhaled in relief. But then, surprisingly, it re-intensified as it made its way east across the state. Mandatory evacuations were issued for all low-lying areas and trailer parks in Palm Beach County. The marina issued an evacuation notice which meant that we were "staying at our own risk." Though many liveaboards heeded the warning and evacuated, I did not consider this an option. Most shelters and hotels would not take pets; besides, who would save the boat if a line chafed through or a piling failed. Ed seemed confident in the preparations we had made, and my confidence in Ed was unfailing. Clive would weather the storm with Vaughan and Cindy, on their boat. All things considered—we were ready.

The first warning gust arrived early on October 24, and I was startled as the boat lurched violently. Kia's nails scraped along the cabin sole, and she slid into the settee with a thud. Another gust, the boat strained hard against her dock lines; the ropes stretched taut, screeching like a rusty hinge.

"Kia, come here, pup, come on. Up! Up!" I had to get her into my berth; she'd be safe in the cushioned bunk.

Kia bounded into the cabin and onto the bed, then she hunkered into a corner and sat huddled stiff and shivering. I felt terrible; I should have gotten her out of here—now it was too late. The wind howled steady and beat against the hull and rig with a vengeance. My confidence wavered in the angry wind. I climbed into the bunk and drew Kia to my side, trying to comfort her. The boat heeled; I looked out from the portlight—*water*—and across—*sky*; we had to be tipped at least forty-five degrees. This was insane. I needed to know how hard the wind was blowing.

I scrambled to the companionway, and slowly slid open the hatch; the wailing intensified. Like a turtle from its shell, I poked my head out, trying to glimpse for just a second the world beyond the safety of my hull; the wind stung as microscopic bits of matter and sand tore into my skin. Like a scene from of the *Wizard of Oz*, I watched as a three foot section of someone's boat soared past; I raised an arm protectively overhead and ducked. Just then the boat lurched, and I was thrown hard against the side of the companionway. The immediate and intense pain would leave a huge bruise on my back along my ribs. Gingerly, I regained my foothold, then removed the cover from the wind gauge—126 knots; the wind was gusting to around 140 miles per hour! I looked toward the park: palm trees laid flat; the small kiosks that lined the boardwalk by the marina were in shambles. And this was just the beginning? I ducked back down to the relative safety of my boat and closed the hatch.

Tea-time. I placed the kettle on the stove, adjusted the pot clamps, set out a mug and was reaching for the sugar when the phone rang; I glanced at the caller ID —Dad. There was a lull in the wind and it seemed as good a time as any to try and allay his concerns.

"Hi, Dad," I answered overly cheery. "How are you?"

"All right," he replied cautiously. "More important, how are you? How are things there?"

"Oh, me…good—really good. You know, they blow things way out of proportion in the news."

"Really," he sounded relieved.

"Yeah, definitely. I mean, here I am, on the boat. I'm making tea as we speak—oh, shit!" The boat lurched, and the tin of sugar went flying across the cabin. The mug smashed on the galley floor, reminding once again that ceramics don't belong on a boat.

"What's going on—are you okay?" he asked, voice tinged with panic.

"Yeah, I'm fine. The wind blew the boat over a bit, and the sugar spilled all over the place. No big deal. I just have to clean it up, that's all."

I managed to lull my dad into a sense of calm. If I could casually talk about spilt sugar and cleaning it up, then surely all must be okay. With promises to call later in the day, I managed to get off the phone as the wind began in earnest. The boat reared and strained like a wild horse trying to break free. It rolled and tossed; books fell from their shelves; I hurtled about the cabin, catching, grabbing, then placing things on the floor just before they toppled. The storm raged for almost two hours and then suddenly it was quiet; there was an eerie stillness and then bits of sun glinted in through the portlights.

Tentatively, I pulled back the hatch and climbed out into the bright light of day. A mass of storm clouds hovered in the distance, foreshadowing what was yet to come. Around me—chaos, destruction, pilings broken, boats half submerged, boats sunk still tethered in their slips. *Nini* was okay, though; Ed surfaced and looked around; others appeared. It was like a "day after" scenario—people creeping slowly out of their shelters to see what was left of the world. And what was left? Solid concrete docks had been torn apart; at least ten boats had sunk, including a large tugboat; and perhaps twenty or so others had suffered catastrophic damage. The electricity was out; we had no running water; and we were sitting in the eye of the storm.

A steady crowd of people flowed down the dock. "Where's everyone going?" I called out.

"Getting out of here," someone answered.

"Where to?"

"The functional hall—it's concrete; we'll be safe there."

I looked over at Ed to gauge his reaction. He raised an eyebrow, and I shrugged. If the second half was no worse than the first, we could make it through out here. But I didn't want to put Kia through that. I looked up and saw Clive and Cindy hurrying our way.

"You too, Clive. You guys are going?"

"Ya. Too dangerous—we lost a cleat; almost lost the boat—not worth it. You should come too. Don't be stubborn."

"I can't, Clive." I glanced in Ed's direction. "I have to stay, but could you please take Kia with you. She's afraid."

"Of course I'll take her. Ag shame—poor Kia—your mother's crazy. Don't worry; I'll take care of you," he said and took her leash. He smiled at me sadly, then looking up at the approaching clouds said, "Sorry, gotta go."

When minutes later the wind began to howl, I was caught off guard. I'd boarded *Nini* to give Ed a hand with the lines and then it was too late to leave; *Gypsy Spirit* would have to ride out the storm alone. Deep within the *Nini*'s belly, I felt safe and very far removed.

"I can't help feeling like something is trying to stop me from going sailing," I said.

"This storm was sent for you?"

"No, not just the storm, Ed. This hurricane season has been crazy. And what about the boat—why does everything keep breaking? And don't tell me I have to pay my dues. I think I've long since paid them."

"Okay, so someone has cast the evil eye on your boat," Ed said somewhat sarcastically.

"Maybe…I wouldn't rule it out."

By four o'clock the storm was over, and a cold dry air mass had settled in. My neighbors returned from the shelter to see if their boats had survived—many hadn't, but at least no one had been hurt. Andrew's dog, Frances, a large German Shepard named after hurricane Frances, was blown off the dock into the water, and Andrew went in after the dog, but they were rescued. Clive brought Kia home. I bundled up as best I could in a wool sweater and wind breaker: no electricity, no heat. It would be a long night.

Several days later, with power restored, life slowly returned to normal. My engine was still at Walter's shop. Ed and I passed the days making small improvements to the boats. He added drains in *Gypsy Spirit*'s cockpit and a water intake, so I could fill the water tank from the deck. I made book shelves, and Ed installed them. We sewed military style hammocks: one for *Nini* and one for *Gypsy Spirit*, and we repaired *Nini*'s lee cloths.

A good deal of our time, at least in the evening, was spent at the Tiki bar drinking copious amounts of tequila, which is odd in that I am not a drinker and normally only partake in the odd glass of wine at a wedding or some such occasion. Yet I'd somehow convinced myself that through sheer force of will I could drink Ed under the table. My only source of pride comes from knowing that I was never wheeled home in a dock cart, as had happened to many a sailor before me. No, one way or another, I made it to my boat—or *thereabouts*—on my own two feet.

Weekends most often found us in downtown West Palm. Ed and Pirate Pete had become good friends, and by that time

Pete had warmed to me as well. The three of us would go out for dinner at O'Shea's on Clematis, then to one of the local nightspots; or we'd get pizza and enjoy an outdoor concert on the plaza. Ed would spend the night complaining that he was unable to attract women, while in all reality he made no effort. Most nights he sat with me, deep in conversation about one thing or another, oblivious to or at least seemingly oblivious to everyone else around. Pete meanwhile embarked on a campaign to get me to go out with him. For the most part, he was teasing, enjoying how easy it was to get me flustered. I was able to fend off his playful advances till one evening when the two of us were having coffee on my boat, after Ed had gone to bed.

"So why won't you go out with me?"

"The truth—you want the truth?"

"Yes."

"Will you promise not to tell anyone?"

"Who am I going to tell?" he asked.

"Never mind—just promise."

"Okay," he said laughing. "Now tell me."

I hesitated for a second…"I have a crush on Ed," I whispered, unable to even say the words aloud.

"And?" he asked.

"And what?"

"And, what are you going to do about it?"

"Nothing—what's there to do about it? If he was interested, he'd make a move."

"What kind of cowardly bullshit is this? I thought you were a cool sailor girl, not a cloister cookie."

"What's a *cloister cookie?*"

"A convent school girl—all prim and proper."

"That's funny; I went to an all-girl catholic school."

Pete roared with laughter. "Well, that explains a lot. Listen if you want him, you have to do something about it."

"Like what?"

"Tell him. Tell him tonight. After I leave, go over there, climb onto his boat, and jump on him."

Now it was my turn to laugh. "Yeah, right, there is no way on earth I'd do that."

"You will, or I'll tell him."

"You can't—you promised."

"I don't care. Either you tell him tonight, or I'll tell him tomorrow. "

My jaw fell, and with that Pete hugged me goodnight and motored off into the darkness.

I hadn't believed he would do it, but Pete followed through on his threat. Ed and I were on my boat the next day and had just finished a late lunch. I handed up two mugs of steaming coffee and joined him in the cockpit.

"Strange thing, Pete says you have a *crush* on me."

I choked on my coffee and then laughed. "Really, did he use those exact words?" I was buying time, trying to think of a way to spin the situation.

"Ya, pretty much. He said you wouldn't go out with him because you had a *crush* on me."

"Oh...well, now I feel bad. I hope I didn't hurt his feelings, but I couldn't think of any other way to put him off. I told him I was into you so that he wouldn't ask me out anymore.

I hope you don't mind." Was it my imagination or did Ed seem slightly disappointed?

"No, that's okay. I was just surprised."

"Good surprised or bad surprised?"

"It was unexpected, that's all," he said, abruptly ending the conversation. And if I'd entertained any thoughts of making a move, I put them aside that instant.

Just before Thanksgiving the brand new, rebuilt engine was installed, and Ed and I began preparations for a combination sea trial–sailing lesson. We would set sail aboard *Gypsy Spirit* on a two-day, off-shore trip to Saint Augustine—my first actual sail. While in Saint Augustine, we'd haul the boat, paint the bottom, then sail back to West Palm and set off for the Bahamas.

"Come on, Kia girl," I called, and we ran toward the park for a last potty run. By the time we returned, Ed was on my boat. The engine was running, and Clive was holding the last line securing boat to dock.

"Hurry up," Ed called. "Time and tide."

I climbed aboard as Kia hopped up onto the deck and took her place by Ed's side. He put the boat in reverse and began backing out of the slip.

"Bye, Clive. Thank you." I waved.

We reached the turning basin by Peanut Island. Ed looked toward the still-turbulent sea. "I think we'll open the sail once we're out the inlet," he said.

I nodded in agreement, but at that point I'd have agreed to anything. My eyes were focused on the elephants on the horizon, and my heart pounded loudly, drowning out almost all else; it sounded as though Ed were talking to me from a far-off place. English Mike had warned me about the elephants. If you see a flat line on the horizon, the seas are calm. If however, you see what looks like a line of marching elephants, you can expect some pretty big seas. We reached the jetty, and the boat began rearing and diving—not too bad, though, and we continued. But the further we got, the larger the seas. I looked back toward the inlet, which already seemed so far away; by this time the boat was literally riding up one side of a wave and crashing down the other. I looked at Ed. He seemed calm but absorbed. Kia was at his side, trembling. He noticed me watching him.

"It will get better once the sails go up," he said.

I was no longer convinced, and I didn't want to be there; I wanted to go back.

"Maybe we should go back and try again in a few days?" I suggested.

"Why? It's fine. Listen, can you do something for me? I need your help," he said.

"What?" I asked.

"I need you to take the helm," he said.

I didn't want to move, but he needed my help. So I got up and, holding on tightly, made my way over to the helm.

"Watch the compass; try to hold a course of eighty degrees."

I nodded and grasped the wheel. It was harder than it looked. We'd ride up a wave and get thrown off course as we crashed down. Then I'd have to overcompensate to get us back on course.

"Turn the boat to starboard. Try to hold it nose to wind. I am going to raise the main sail."

We headed due east, directly into the waves. The main sail flapped, wildly, loudly, luffing about in the wind. Moments later, with the sail up, Ed returned to the cockpit and took the helm.

"I've got it now," he said.

"I thought you said it would get better once the sail was up?"

"It will once we turn north. Right now we have to head into the wind to get out far enough."

I didn't want to be there. I felt trapped and a terrible thought occurred to me: I was doomed to be on this boat for the next two days.

"Ed."

Nothing.

"Ed!"

"Hmm." He was absorbed.

"Ed, I don't think I like sailing," I said.

"What?"

"I said, I don't think I like sailing."

"Don't you dare," he said.

"What?"

"Don't do this. Not after all the time I've spent waiting for you. Don't you dare tell me you don't like sailing," he said.

I thought he'd say we could go back once he heard that I was miserable, but he didn't. He was determined that we continue. Other than demanding that we turn back, which I considered for about one second, my only apparent means of escape was sleep, and I felt so very tired.

"Do you mind if I lay down for a bit?" I asked.

"No, that's a good idea. Go ahead," he said.

I felt guilty, leaving him to handle everything alone. But at that moment, my need to be gone outweighed my guilt. I took a last look at Kia, who was hunkered down next to Ed, and had calmed under his soothing touch. They were both okay. I lay down in the cockpit facing the seat-back on the port side and hooked my left leg up and over the seat to keep from falling as we tossed about. I closed my eyes and felt my leg muscles contract, holding me in place. My body found a rhythm in the madness, and I drifted off. I don't know how much time passed—maybe an hour, maybe more—but I woke to a strange calmness. At first, I didn't move. I didn't want Ed to know I was awake and perhaps ask me to do something, but at last I opened my eyes. Something was definitely different; instead of chaos, we were riding smoothly along the waves. The boat felt solid and moved with purpose. A rhythmic swoosh had replaced the hum of the engine. I turned my head to look at Ed, and to my surprise he wasn't at the helm. The cockpit was empty except for me. I sat up in alarm and scanned the boat. Ed was seated on the forward deck with Kia. The main sail was up, and the jib, unfurled. We were on a beam reach, gently riding the waves as they propelled us on to our destination. Why wasn't he at the helm? Then it dawned on me—the autopilot. So it did work… we had not tried it before. I sat quietly, taking it all in. This was my first actual sail and I was at once amazed, thrilled, humbled, and awed. I felt at one with the boat and the sea and the sky. I felt…alive and didn't want to ruin the moment, but I couldn't wait to tell Ed. I rose tentatively and made my way forward.

"Look, Kia, your mother has finally surfaced. Hello, sleepyhead," Ed said.

"Hi," I said sheepishly.

"How's it going?" he asked.

"Pretty good. I've changed my mind…I like sailing."

"Glad to hear it," he said and smiled.

"The autopilot works?"

"Ya, but we might want to calibrate it."

"How long till we get there?"

"We should arrive sometime late tomorrow night. Why?" he asked.

"This might sound strange, but now I don't want the trip to end."

"Not strange, and don't worry, we still have the trip back."

"And all of the Bahamas and Caribbean." For the first time I understood the thrill of sailing.

We reached the Saint Augustine inlet at three in the morning a day and a half later. It was a quiet night; we entered the harbor by moonlight and anchored north of the Bridge of Lions, by the Castillo de San Marco. My little village looked peaceful in its slumber, and I felt a sense of homecoming. In the morning, we'd go through the bridge and over to Oasis Boatyard.

"Are you coming down? It's late," I asked.

"No. I'm not comfortable with the holding. I'm going to keep an eye out. You go get some rest."

"What? All night? You are going to stay out there all night."

"It's almost morning. The sun will be up soon, but yes."

My feelings were hurt. I took Ed's decision to remain outside as rejection, even though he said it was for our safety. Surely he was telling me that a cold night on a hard bench was preferable to sharing my bunk.

We hauled the boat, sanded the bottom, applied the antifouling, and launched just before the boatyard closed for Thanksgiving holiday. We invited Sam for turkey dinner and celebrated the holiday in the lift bay at Oasis, and then it was time to turn around and head south.

We listened to NOAA weather radio: another system was moving up the coast. This time Ed was the one to suggest the Intercoastal; the wind would be on our nose the entire trip, but at least we wouldn't be battling the seas. The first ten miles were great; the engine ran smoothly; the wind wasn't bad. I was just settling in when suddenly, out of the blue, the engine started making a terrible grinding noise, and then there was a loud bang. My heart almost stopped—this couldn't be happening…again. I glanced at Ed; our eyes met for the briefest of seconds, long enough for me to see the hint of hopeless despair already threatening. He pulled the engine stop, then ducked below to survey the damage. I was frozen in place; I didn't want to know—not yet. I wanted just a few precious seconds more to believe that all our efforts had not been in vain. He returned as I was setting the anchor; I didn't have to ask; he looked defeated.

"Dropped a connecting rod—again. The block is shattered. Strange though—it's the same rod as last time."

"I'll call TowBoat," I said mechanically, still in shock.

"Ya, go ahead, but let's have tea first." He sounded as numb as I felt, and I knew it was over. When the guy who states arrogantly that he's not a TowBoat US kind of guy says, "Ya, go ahead," you knew the battle was lost.

Maybe my boat was cursed. Working out the kinks was one thing; this had to be more than kinks. Sailors are a superstitious lot, and there are probably as many superstitions as there are boats on the water: don't board with your left foot first; don't look back when embarking on a voyage; redheads are bad luck unless you speak to them first; it's bad luck to have bananas on board; bad luck to have flowers on board; bad luck to start a journey on a Friday; bad luck to have a woman on board; and, most of all, it's bad luck to rename a boat. What if the person renaming the boat is a woman: does that cancel out the bad luck or make it worse? I purchased a boat called *Manatee* and renamed her *Gypsy Spirit*, and before that there had been another name: I could still see its ghost, the impression unfaded though the letters had long since been removed. I made sure to follow proper renaming protocol. I'd had a christening ceremony and had broken a bottle of champagne (expensive champagne) over the bow. But what about my predecessors: Had they done everything right? Was I dealing with residual bad luck? Okay, now I knew it for sure—I was losing my mind, sitting here seriously considering bad karma, evil eyes, and archaic superstitions as viable explanations. I had to get a grip.

TowBoat US arrived forty-five minutes later, and returned *Gypsy Spirit* to the Municipal Marina in Saint Augustine; we were right back where we started four months ago.

I called my dad. "It's over," I said.

It was time to take Ed home to Nini. We drove to West Palm in silence—there was nothing left to say. We had run out of options, ideas, and hope. Four hours later we were seated at the Tiki bar. Clive shook his head in disbelief.

"The connecting rod again—how is that possible?" he asked.

I shrugged.

"Why is everyone so glum?" I heard a familiar voice and turned to see Greg approaching. Greg was a friend of Clive's who'd started a nonprofit organization called Lagoon Keepers. The primary function of the organization was to keep the waterway clear of all hazards to navigation. Early on he'd done the patrols alone, funding the project himself, and now Lagoon Keepers had grown into a sizable operation. I went with him once when the Coast Guard had called and reported a large piling floating in the waterway.

"It's over, Greg." I told him what happened.

He was quiet for a moment. "Hmm...Did I ever tell you that my old boat had a Perkins engine?"

I shook my head.

"I've been saving it, knew it might come in handy someday. It doesn't run, but maybe you can strip mine down and take the parts you need."

"You're going to give me your engine?"

He nodded and smiled.

I Met Someone

November 2006

Oasis Boatyard
Saint Augustine, Florida

"Is something wrong? You sound different," Ed said, ten minutes into our weekly call.

"Yes and no..."

"Uh-oh."

"It's not bad...You're probably going to laugh at me when I tell you," I said.

"Okay."

"It's just that...I...um...I met someone."

Silence.

"Ed...Are you there?"

"Ya...you met someone and...?"

"Well, nothing really—nothing's happened...and you and I—we're not together or anything, and I'm not cheating on you. But for some strange reason, I feel like I am."

"Funny that you say that because, for some strange reason, I feel that way too, although I know I have no right to feel that way." He was quiet for a moment. "So what does this mean? Do you still want me to come? Are we still going cruising?"

"Of course…of course we are. I just needed you to know, that's all. Everything's the same."

"Cool. In a way, I'm glad you brought this up."

"You are? Why?" I asked.

"I didn't want to say anything before, but I met someone too. I was thinking of asking her to come sailing."

It felt as though all the air had been sucked from my lungs. "Hey, that's great," I managed to say.

"I'm glad you're okay with the idea. Hey, wouldn't it be cool if the four of us went sailing together?"

"Yeah, that would be really nice."

I was more confused than ever, but I knew for my own peace of mind and sanity I should tell Ben it was over—no matter how upset he got. It would be hard, mostly because we would still see each other every day. What had I been thinking—getting involved with a man who lived in a motel, barely worked, had no car, no driver's license, and had what I'd now learned to be a pretty serious drug and alcohol problem? The obvious answer to that question was that I wasn't thinking. I was as much a wreck on the inside as my boat was on the outside.

Ed visiting with the pigs in the Exumas

Bahamas Bound... At Last

February 2006

West Palm Beach, Florida
To The Bahamas

At long last, almost seven months to the day after I'd first arrived, I said goodbye to my family and friends. We gathered at the Tiki bar: my dad and Amal had come down from Boston; Clive was there, and Vaughan and Cindy, Pirate Pete and little Skippy, Alaska Bill, Captain Gary, Budweiser Bill; and I was sure Diesel Bob was there in spirit. There were well-wishers and advice-givers, and I was sad to say goodbye.

I hugged my dad, and we walked toward the boat. I didn't know what to say, and so I remained silent.

After a moment he began, "I remember when I left for France…almost fifty years ago. My sister came to the port to see me off. I can still see her standing there…waving." He shook his head clearing away the old memory. "I don't know why I just thought of that, but I think I know now how she felt that day. Take care of yourself...please."

"I will, Dad. Don't worry. I love you."

I gave Kia some Dramamine, hoisted the mainsail, and followed Ed through the Lake Worth inlet. I was pleased with how easy it had been to raise the anchor and with the absence of smoke from the exhaust when I'd started the engine. These were good signs, and I'd become an expert on signs.

"*Gypsy Spirit*...*Gypsy Spirit*...*Nini*—over." Ed's voice startled me.

I picked up the receiver. "*Nini*, this is *Gypsy Spirit*—over."

"How's it going back there?"

"Great, everything's fine," I said, somewhat surprised by the lack of incident.

It was all too simple: no drama, no mishap, no frayed nerves, and by noon we'd reached the Gulf Stream, where the sea undulated like taffy, a deep cobalt blue, and there was not a glimpse of land in sight. The boat rolled a bit in the large residual swell and light wind, but as the day went on and the miles passed, it calmed, and I watched the sun set into a flat peaceful sea. The months of uncertainty, stress, and fear dissolved as I marveled at the fiery orb on the horizon. I was filled with a most indescribable joy, a happiness and content that I had never— and have not since—experienced. We reached the Bahamas Bank just before midnight. The transition from deep sea to shallows was sudden, and before I knew it, we were sailing along in depths of only twelve to fourteen feet. I followed Ed, keeping his masthead light in sight, which could easily be mistaken for one of the millions of stars, glittering just overhead through the inky blackness, like fairy dust upon a velvet sky.

I was tired beyond exhaustion, but the thrill of finally being in the Bahamas sustained me, and with several hours of darkness yet to go, I heaped blankets into the cockpit, creating a little nest where I could hunker and still keep watch. I was careful not to close my eyes, not even for a second. I was afraid I'd fall asleep, and my boat would drift away unnoticed into the darkness. I sat up, lit a cigarette, then went below and put the kettle on—anything to keep busy and awake. Finally I saw the faintest hint of light—not so much light as a lessening of the dark, a gradual changeover from black to gray then gray-blue. In the distance, a momentary glimpse of land appeared and then was gone; at first I thought it a trick of the light or the imaginings of my tired eyes, but a few seconds later, it reappeared—and this time it remained. As the sun rose higher, the island of Great Sale Cay became clearly visible.

We anchored, and I took in my surroundings. It was not postcard perfect—no sandy beach and no swaying palms. Rather, the island was long and rocky and covered in low-lying dense brush. We'd anchored in sea grass, which gave the water a dark murky hue, but I didn't care; I was in the Bahamas. I also didn't care that the water looked cold and uninviting and that the air temperature was barely out of the sixties; I held my nose and my breath, waved at Ed who was on deck watching me, and jumped in with a splash, clothes and all. Ed captured the moment on his digital camera. The moment did not last long; the water was so cold it hurt.

Great Sale Cay is a deserted island; ours were the only boats in the anchorage. We motored ashore, made landfall barefoot and leash-less, and then set off on a long walk. Kia swam and dug in the wet sand; she chased little blue crabs, and pranced in the shallows. I watched Kia, savoring her freedom, as I followed Ed along the shore.

"What more could anyone ask for, hmm, Kia?" I murmured softly, taking in the warm sun and the absolute beauty of our solitude. The final blessing of my day came when I realized that I had a cell phone signal and could call my family and let them know we'd crossed safely, and all was well.

The wind howled when I woke in predawn gloom to the wild rocking of the boat. I climbed the companionway, holding tight lest I lose my footing, and glanced over at *Nini*. Ed was busy on deck; he saw me and waved.

"*Gypsy Spirit...Gypsy Spirit...Nini*—over." His voice came over the VHF.

"Good morning, *Nini*. What's up?" I said trying to sound cheery.

"We have to get out of here," he said.

"What?" I asked in a groggy, pre-coffee haze.

"We have to get out of here now. The wind shifted. If our anchors drag, we'll end up on the beach."

"Alright," I answered without enthusiasm. I wanted to crawl back inside and curl up in a warm blanket, but instead I started the engine, put on my gloves, and motored forward. I raced to the bow to pull in the anchor, but by the time I reached the foredeck, the wind had blown me back, and the anchor line was stretched tight. I tried again and again till I was winded, my arms ached, and my thigh muscles burned from the exertion.

"Ed, I can't do it. The wind keeps blowing me back," I said into the receiver.

"Okay."

"Okay what?" I asked confused.

"You have two options," he said, and I listened, although I was already prepared to choose whichever option involved Ed coming to the rescue.

"Yes." I waited for His Brilliance to speak.

"It's simple: do it or don't—your choice," he said.

"What?" Not what I expected to hear.

"Do it or don't do it—it's up to you," he repeated.

Absurdly, it made perfect sense. I had two choices. I didn't ask what happened if I chose the second option.

"Okay…here goes." I put the boat in forward, revved the engine, and gunned it far past the anchor; then raced forward and began pulling in the slack. I pulled hard and fast while the boat heaved beneath me like a mechanical bull. I'd pulled up all the line and most of the chain by the time the wind and waves caught the boat. I secured the chain, then waited for a wave to break free the anchor. The swell came quickly, and the boat was free. Once clear of the anchorage, I hauled in the rest of the chain and secured the anchor. Winded but feeling great, I motored out after Ed, and soon the sun was shining. I had just gotten the first glimpse of what I was capable of.

We were on our way to Powell Cay, only forty miles from Great Sale, which no longer seemed like a great distance considering the hundred and ten miles we traveled to get from West Palm to Great Sale Cay. Ed was stressed out, I could tell, and I wondered if perhaps my inexperience was beginning to weigh on him.

Powell Cay was exactly what I'd imagined a Bahamian Island would be...beautiful beaches on the Atlantic and a tranquil bay. I walked along the beach, trailing behind Ed, watching him scavenge for conch, watching Kia as she watched him. The deserted island thing was new for her—and me: no leash, no commands to come or heel or stay. She was free to do whatever she pleased, and what pleased her most was prancing in the shallows, leaping after the tiny glistening fish.

A deserted island, a boy, a girl, a dog, a sunset and two sailboats—this was paradise, right? Not exactly—something had changed between us, and I wasn't sure what. Ed was distant; the easy camaraderie of the states was gone; all conversation now revolved around sailing, heavy weather tactics, and mechanical malfunctions. To further complicate matters, I felt ungrateful. I should have been thrilled. Ed was a wonderful teacher, a friend; he was someone I could trust. What more did I want? Nothing, actually, if it meant jeopardizing what we had now. Ah, well, tomorrow we'd be off to Green Turtle Cay and our first taste of Bahamian civilization. I was looking forward to a cold drink at Sundowners.

Gentle hills and narrow winding lanes dotted with pretty pastel cottages slowly came into view as I adjusted the focus on my binoculars. Small white ferries zipped through sparkling aquamarine water, delivering residents and tourists to and from the larger island of Great Abaco. It was a tropical fairytale village. We anchored in New Plymouth Harbor, and then made our way into town, to the Customs and Immigration office, where we cleared in before setting off to explore the island. Green Turtle Cay was founded by loyalists during the Revolutionary War, or the War for American Independence as it was called here. Many of the original buildings had survived, including the old jail, and it was a history lover's paradise—a little village frozen in time.

The island is also home to the Potcake, for short—formally known as a Bahamian Potcake or Royal Bahamian Potcake. This breed of dog received that name on account of the rice and pea mixture (a staple of the Bahamian diet) that was scraped from the bottom of pots and fed to stray dogs back in the day. They became an official breed of the Bahamas and Turks and Caicos in the 1970s.

On our first night in Green Turtle, we went to Sundowners, a quaint little bar on the beach by Plymouth Harbor. We ordered tropical cocktails by color: first the red, then the blue, and then another red one; and after a bit the tension between us dissolved. We talked and laughed about all we'd been through to reach this point. We discussed plans for the upcoming week and our trip south. We were deep in conversation when we were interrupted by a newcomer.

"Those your boats out there in the harbor?" asked the middle-aged man who'd just entered the bar. He was obviously a local; everyone seemed to know him.

"Yes, why?" Ed asked.

"We're due for a storm—the *perfect storm*, some say. See how fast the clouds are racing across the sky," he said, pointing.

I looked up. It was true; I felt a shiver run down my spine.

"If I were you, I'd be lookin' for a mooring. You should take those boats into Black Sound."

"Thanks, we will," Ed answered, and then to me, "Tomorrow morning, I'll ride with you. We'll take your boat into the sound and get you on a mooring."

"What about you?"

"Let's get you situated, and then I'll worry about me."

We moved my boat onto the last available mooring in Black Sound, then Ed brought his boat around and anchored.

Sunday morning the front was upon us, and the temperature had dropped; it was raining, and the wind was blowing, but Kia and I were warm, dry, and comfortable inside the boat. It still amazed me how peaceful it could seem below deck even in a gale. Luckily we'd been to shore for a potty run before the storm settled in. I checked the wind gauge: forty-six knots. This was definitely one of those *hunker down* days that sailors speak of. I hadn't heard from Ed and hoped that he was similarly comfortable on his boat.

"Maybe I should bake some bread." Kia stared without expression; she knew when I was talking to her and when I was talking to myself. I'd like to say that I whipped up a perfect loaf of bread from scratch on my very first try, but actually, I whipped up a perfect loaf of bread from a mix on my very first try. The lovely aroma of baking bread was just filling the cabin when Ed called.

"How are you doing there?" he asked slightly out of breath.

"Fine—really well actually. I just made some bread. Would you like to come over?" I was proud to sound so nonchalant and efficient in the face of this harrowing storm. It never occurred to me that Ed might be having troubles.

"Ya, maybe in a bit. I just dragged—ripped straight through the anchorage—had to recover two anchors and get the boat running before we were impaled."

"Oh my god, Ed. Are you okay?"

"Yes, yes."

"What do you mean impaled?"

"Remember that beautiful Ketch, with the shiny black hull and long bowsprit?" he asked.

"Yes."

"Well, *Nini* was aiming for it. Anyway, it's over now...I found a mooring, and I can finally relax."

"Ed, I'm so sorry. I feel bad...but actually, better you than me," I said teasing. "I mean can you imagine...?"

"Ya...no, I don't want to. What was that you said about baking bread?"

"The loaf is in the oven, should be ready in less than an hour."

"Cool. I'll be over in a while; we can take the hound ashore as well."

Luckily we'd heeded the warning to take shelter. Other than Ed's dragging episode we weathered the storm unscathed and as soon as the skies cleared we raised our sails and followed the sun. For the next several days we hopped from island to island, down the Abacos chain south, in search of warmer weather. We anchored at Great Guana Cay, famous for Nippers and their Sunday pig roasts; we sailed to Marsh Harbor for supplies and another sailing lesson, then on to Man of War Cay—a picture perfect island of sun and sea and swaying palms. The island is home to the Albury boat-building family. We anchored within the well-protected harbor, and then set off to explore the bustling main street lined with cafes, restaurants, canvas shops and boatyards.

"I'm curious," Ed said over coffee in the evening. "Are you just following me from place to place?"

"What do you mean?" I asked.

"I mean, do you know how to use your GPS or are you just following me?"

"I can't believe you are asking me that. But to answer your second question, I have been following you—just easier."

"Ya, don't do that; always navigate your own course," he said, still unconvinced. "You're sure you know how to use it?"

"You know what—we're going to Lynyard Cay tomorrow, right?"

"Uh-huh."

"I'll lead the way. You follow me this time," I said.

"Okay, but better yet, I'll give you an hour head start."

"Sounds good. Well, I think I'll turn in now—want to get an early start."

Ed took the hint and returned to *Nini* a few minutes later. I scrambled below, pulled away the settee cushion, and removed a ziplocked bag of equipment manuals and warranties from within the storage locker. I opened the bag and began sorting through the damp moldy pages: sink faucet warranty, radio manual, battery monitor documentation, wind instrumentation, autopilot manual; and then I found it—the manual for my Garmin GPS handheld. I was going to have to learn sometime.

Why not now? I put the coffee on to brew, knowing it was going to be a long night.

Several hours later I fell into my bunk, exhausted but reasonably confident in my knowledge of the workings of the GPS; actually I was surprised at how intuitively it functioned and felt somewhat silly for having put this off for so long. Tomorrow I would put my knowledge to the test; most of the routes we'd travelled so far had involved one, two, maybe three waypoints. I'd carefully entered, checked, then double-checked ten separate points entered by degree, minute, and second on the zigzag route to Lynyard Cay; among reef, inlet, and sandy shoal there could be no margin for error.

I rose early, organized my charts and navigational equipment, then waved goodbye to Ed, who was sipping coffee and watching as usual. I felt self-conscious as I sailed out of the anchorage but didn't want to turn and look, even though I was sure he was staring after me, looking to see if I was going the right way. For the most part, the trip went well, but I got confused between the Pelican Harbor waypoint and the Pelican Cay waypoint and ended up going in circles for what seemed like an eternity. Finally I reached Lynyard Cay and anchored, feeling both relieved and elated; this was to me a major accomplishment, a far cry from when I'd wondered what a waypoint looked like. Day by day, as my experience and skills increased, so did my confidence in my abilities. Ed arrived just about an hour after me, and we ferried ashore.

"How did it go?" he asked

"Great—just one little hiccup. I got confused when I couldn't seem to reach Pelican Harbor waypoint."

"Ya, I saw that. I was afraid that you were going to run aground, but I didn't want to call and distract you."

"It was a mess, but then I realized what I did wrong. I was following a route and because I hadn't gotten close enough to the waypoint, it wouldn't go on to the next one. I finally canceled the route and hit 'Go To' to reach each of the next points."

"Good thinking. I don't use routes myself. Like you saw, they can get confusing."

We followed a path across the island to the ocean. On the shore we found a deserted camp crafted from bits of flotsam and driftwood and decorated with seashells. There was a tattered hammock strung between two palms and draped in seaweed, a makeshift table, and a couple of broken chairs. There was an old sign that read Greg's Pub, and had it not been for the bits of charcoal still warm in the fire pit, I might have imagined that we'd happened upon a pirate's camp from long ago. A warm breeze blew in quite suddenly from the south and seemed to foretell the sultry days and nights that were to come. We had happened upon a magical place, and I wanted the night to last forever. But soon it was time to go—time to make ready for tomorrow's journey.

We hauled anchor on Saturday, February 18, bound for Allen's Cay in the Exumas, a distance of approximately ninety miles. I thought I would be nervous as we left the safety of the bank for the ocean and major shipping routes, yet two hours into the trip, I found myself sitting back, completely relaxed, gazing out over the vast ocean and watching the sun sink slowly into the horizon. Kia was still unhappy about doing her business on deck but being the amazingly resourceful being that she is, she'd found a solution to the problem. The first time I'd seen her do it I couldn't believe my eyes. She'd actually backed herself up against the stern rail, hung her bottom over the transom and did her business overboard. That happened when we were crossing over from the United States and thankfully she'd felt comfortable enough that it just became routine.

"Good girl Kia. Very good girl," I said praising her. She finished and joined me in the cockpit. We sat together looking out over the ocean, savoring the moment.

Around midnight I spotted what looked like a giant moving chandelier but was obviously a cruise ship; it passed quietly to my stern; then a cargo ship, and another—we were crossing the Providence Channel, a major shipping route, and the flurry of activity helped me remain awake and alert. We reached the Fleming Channel shortly after sunrise. Ed had timed our departure so that we'd arrive and have the sun to navigate our way around the coral heads and across the channel. With the sun lighting our way, they were easy enough to avoid, and long before sunset we'd anchored at Allen's Cay.

The Exumas remain an exotic yet underexplored blur in my memory; for although we sailed through the chain of more than three hundred islands, our goal was to reach Georgetown by March, in time for the regatta and the arrival of Ed's friends and, later, Tanya. The distance between islands was greater in the Exumas than in the Abacos and the water had turned from translucent turquoise to glimmering aquamarine.

On Allen's Cay, like a scene out of *Jurassic Park*, giant iguanas emerged from the shrubbery, and converged on the beach. They were curious of the visitors who'd landed on their island.

We stopped for the day at Staniel Cay and took a dinghy ride to Thunderball Cave, where the movies *Thunderball* and *Splash* were filmed. We dove into the cave and I tried to photograph the myriad of fish shimmering like jewels in the sunlight that poured in from a crevice in the ceiling.

We visited Big Majors Cay, an island populated by chubby pink pigs that swam out to meet our dinghy. And we spent a night anchored at Blackpoint, perhaps my favorite settlement in all the Bahamas. Coming ashore on Blackpoint was like stepping into a postcard: the water was clear; the sand was white; bougainvillea grew wild; and the shoreline was dotted with the cutest, brightly colored cottages. But once again it was time to move on; we left Blackpoint for Little Galliot Cay, our point of departure for Georgetown.

I will remember the Exumas as the most beautiful part of my trip, a wild and sometimes remote paradise to which I hope to return someday, but I'll also remember it with sadness for all it could have been. My feelings for Ed could no longer be denied, but being the coward I was, I was afraid to say anything—partly out of pride, but mostly out of fear of losing what we had. I remained silent, sadly watching the days pass.

A low-pressure system moved in, bringing with it gusty winds and rough seas; I knew Ed would probably choose a hideously chaotic moment to call and say we had to be underway; when he hailed me a short while later, I knew what was coming.

"*Gypsy Spirit*...*Gypsy Spirit*...*Nini*—over."

"*Nini*, this is *Gypsy Spirit*—up one."

"Up one."

"*Nini*, are you there?"

"Ya, listen. We've got to get out of here," he said predictably.

"I don't want to; it's miserable."

"The winds are clocking; it's not going to be safe. Come on, it won't be so bad once we get going."

I resigned myself to the fact that we were leaving and started the engine. The anchor came up easily, and moments later with Ed leading the way, we headed toward Galliot Cut. *Nini* looked like a rocking horse, rearing and diving as Ed made his way through the cut.

"Great, we're in for a rockin' rollercoaster ride from hell," I called down to Kia, who stared balefully up at me from the salon. "It's for your own safety, pup. Believe me, you'll be much happier down there." No sooner had I spoken, the boat reared abruptly and then pitched. The next wave curled high over the bow, sending a torrent of water crashing into the cockpit and my coffee mug smashing onto the deck. Kia's nails scraped along the cabin floor as she slid from front to back. Pots and pans clanged, swinging wildly. An army of angry trolls had taken possession of the boat and were busily banging and tossing everything within reach. At least that's what it sounded like.

"It will calm down in a few minutes, pup." Kia looked up at the sound of my voice. "Good girl. It's okay—it's gonna be okay." I looked up, trying to see if the sea looked calmer ahead, and saw *Nini*'s sails suddenly unfurl and Ed begin to tack back and forth through the narrow opening of the cut.

"What the heck," I spoke aloud. His engine had been temperamental lately, and from time to time he'd had to shut it down. "Perfect timing." One stress-filled half hour later, we made it to open water. But there was still a good chop, and we were running directly into the wind.

After several hours of rolling, bouncing, gusting winds, autopilot that wouldn't cooperate, a full bladder, hunger, thirst, Kia crying, and things flying around down below, I had had it. I was angry with Ed and his magnetic fascination with foul weather, angry with the author of the sailing book who suggested I take the helm while my crew hoists the sails; most of all, I was angry with myself, and I promised I would never be out in conditions like this again. I understood that Ed's outlook was different; he came from the perspective of one who'd crossed oceans and knew that "bad weather happened." It was just something you dealt with, but we shouldn't have to deal with it. Ours were short passages; with planning and time, we should have been able to avoid most foul weather.

Eight hours and ten miles later, it didn't seem so bad anymore; I was practically numb. By the time we neared Adderly Cut, I could almost say I was comfortable. We entered the cut, sailed by Lee Stocking Cay, and anchored off Leaf Cay, next to the only other boat I'd seen all day. The chart showed that we'd anchored in an area marked *Poor Holding*. A better spot was just across the way, but that slipped my mind when Ed pulled up to take us ashore. The tiny island of Leaf Cay beckoned. Kia explored the large rocky outcropping and every tidal pool along the shore. I went in for a quick swim, then joined Ed on the beach.

"You might want to get a second anchor ready," Ed said.

"Really, why?" I asked.

"Why not?" he replied tersely.

"I figured, since you mentioned it, there must be a reason, that's all," I responded defensively.

"Does there have to be a reason?"

"No, but you've never mentioned it before. Just seems odd."

"I should have," he said.

"Okay, I have to check the oil too."

Prepare the second anchor and check oil level...there was plenty of time for that. At that moment, I was craving something chocolaty and sweet. I had a tub of marshmallow fluff with a recipe for fudge printed on the container—perfect. I gathered ingredients, mixed and made the fudge. I would let the fudge cool while I checked the oil level. I grabbed a paper towel to wipe the dipstick then opened the engine access cover and stared down into the bilge in shock. It was full of water; soon it would be spilling out onto the cabin floors; the pump hummed but wasn't pumping. I grabbed the VHF transmitter.

"Ed, I have a problem. The bilge pump's not pumping, and the bilge is full."

"Make sure the hose is connected; check the impeller; see if it's blocked, then tighten those packing gland nuts—that's where the water's coming from."

"Okay." I knew all this; why did I call him? I guess I hoped it would be, "Plan A—Ed to the rescue." So much for Plan A. Time for Plan B. First I needed to check the bilge pump. I reached down as far as I could into the bilge, but my arm wasn't long enough, not even when I laid flat on my belly and half-leaned into the bilge. So, instead of disconnecting the pump from the mount at the base, I rocked and tugged at the outlet hose until the pump popped free. The hoses were properly attached and the filter was clear, but still no water pumping out. I couldn't remount the pump, so I set it in the bilge and let it float in the rising water. It was time to take care of the stuffing box and slow or stop the incoming water. I grabbed my two largest wrenches and attached them to the packing gland nuts. I knew I was supposed to loosen one in order to tighten the other but whatever I did just seemed to increase the flow of water.

"*Nini…Nini…Gypsy Spirit*—over," I hailed.

"*Gypsy Spirit*, this is *Nini*," Ed answered.

"Ed, the hoses are attached; the impeller's clear; and I can't tighten the packing nuts."

"All right, can you come get me?" he asked.

Good question—the outboard had been acting up lately. Two sparks plugs and ten minutes of cranking later, I had the answer; the outboard wouldn't start, and we weren't going anywhere.

Plan C—I pulled out my now well-worn volume of Nigel Calder's *Your Boat's Electrical and Mechanical Systems*. I opened the book to the section on bilge pumps. The wind was picking up and with it the seas. I sat on the galley floor. Water sloshed and splashed around in the bilge as the boat rocked from side to side and front to back. I opened the pump per the diagram and cleared some debris from the intake, hoping this would solve the problem; then I reassembled and lowered it into the bilge.

With my fingers crossed, I flipped the switch and—nothing. The pump hummed, but the water level continued to rise.

Okay, Plan D. I began bailing, dumping the water into the sink, where it could run directly to the sea. I put a cup under the stuffing box to catch water before it ran into the bilge. If I emptied the cup every couple of minutes and continued bailing, I'd have a handle on things in about a half hour. Every few minutes I'd stop and check the GPS, hoping I wouldn't see numbers that indicated fluctuation in our position. The wind had really picked up, and the second anchor wasn't ready. Time passed, and the routine continued: empty cup; bail water; check GPS; empty cup; bail water; check GPS…At last, the level was dropping. I bailed, then moved to the GPS…cool. No, wait…

"Oh, shit! We're dragging!" I didn't need the GPS to know, the motion felt different; we were being swept along, beam to current—rapidly.

"*Gypsy Spirit*…*Gypsy Spirit*…You're dragging—watch out—you're heading toward the reef!" Ed's voice rang out from the VHF.

I was on deck in a second, spotlight in hand; white foam glowed less than one hundred feet away and breakers crashed on the reef. I turned the key, pushed the start button, and thrust the boat into forward. I risked running over my anchor line, but at this point it was the best option; I had to clear the shore. With no moon to illuminate the night, I drove in darkness toward Ed's anchor light. There came a sudden *clang-snap*, and I lost steering; then the boat began drifting back toward the reef. I ran to the bow, threw open the anchor locker, and grabbed hold of the Danforth—my largest heaviest anchor—but it was wedged in and wouldn't budge. So I grabbed the Bruce, a smaller plow-style anchor, and dropped it over the bow. I waited to see if it grabbed—no such luck, and time was running out. I got into the anchor locker, grabbed hold of the Danforth, twisted, turned, and wiggled till it came loose. I heaved it out onto the deck, then tossed it over the side, knowing that this was my last chance; I had no more anchors and no steering. I held my breath and waited…the line stretched taut like my nerves and then—it held. It held beautifully.

The boat was now in the middle of the channel, where the current was the strongest, where the holding was poor and the wind had whipped up three to four foot seas. The boat reared and bucked wildly, but for the moment we held fast. I looked at the wind gauge: forty-five knots. I picked up the VHF transmitter, no longer worried about proper radio protocol, no longer caring who was listening.

"Ed, I think I'm okay; the anchor's holding. I'm going below to check the—hold on, what's that?" My attention was drawn to the reef by lights and a woman's screams. I couldn't believe what I was seeing and hearing.

"Ed, that other boat is on the reef; they must have dragged."

"Ya, I saw the guy pulling up anchor. I figured he wanted to move."

"There's a woman; she's waving at me, and she's screaming for help. What do I do?" I asked.

"You can't do anything. Your boat is barely anchored, and your outboard isn't working. Stay put."

"I can see them; they're on the beach. They have a dog too. The guy is getting in his dinghy; he's got a line. I think he's trying to get the boat off the rocks. Listen, I'll call you back in a bit."

I couldn't take my eyes off the man in the dinghy. The sea was turbulent; the wind sweeping; the current churning. I couldn't imagine being out there in a little dinghy. The man was a mere shadow almost swallowed in darkness and though I strained to keep him in sight I didn't want to shine my spotlight and potentially blind him. I watched till he returned to his boat, then I climbed down the companionway to check the bilge. It was quiet below deck. I couldn't hear the howling wind or the crashing waves; even the motion seemed less intense. For a moment I was tempted to curl up in a ball and pretend that none of this was happening. The bilge was full again, most likely because I'd run the engine, and the stuffing box leaked faster when it was running. I bailed for a few minutes then checked the GPS—still holding. I popped my head out to check the status of the other boat. Thankfully they'd managed to get off the rocks. Would I have been able to get my boat off a reef? I hoped I didn't ever have to answer that question. They must not have sustained any significant damage. I went below and continued bailing.

"*Gypsy Spirit*...*Gypsy Spirit*...They're coming straight at you; shine your spotlight on them!" Ed's warning cut through me like a jolt of electricity.

I grabbed the spotlight and leaped up the stairwell. We were only about ten feet apart and closing. The woman was screaming at me.

"Go! Go! *No*!" She waved her arms wildly, gesturing for me to get away. Their dog barked and ran back and forth along the deck. The man was watching, like me, trying to figure out what was going on. I called to them.

"My steering doesn't work, I can't get away." As I spoke our boats collided; my starboard side to his portside. The man jumped onto the deck, climbed over his lifelines and wedged himself between our two boats. I feared he would be crushed as our boats rose and fell with each wave. I grabbed one then another fender and wedged them into the space he'd created with his body. He swung back aboard and released his solar panels before they were crushed between our hulls. We ran from bow to stern, catching railings and lifelines, pushing and shoving to lessen the impact, as the swells drove us into each other.

Then suddenly the man jumped into his cockpit. "I know what's happening," he yelled, then he disengaged his windlass and began letting out line. "I threw my anchor over your anchor line," he said. "When I used the windlass to pull my boat off the shore, my anchor must have caught yours. We're tangled together."

He fed out chain as he explained, and his boat slid slowly down the length of mine. The woman and I continued fending off till their boat was lying off my stern, with about five to seven feet between us. The man joined us.

"Our anchor lines are tangled," he said. "I'm afraid to let out more chain; we could both end up dragging. It's best if we stay this way tonight and sort it out in the morning."

This was our only option, but it was a gamble, and the odds were not with us. If the final anchor dragged, both boats would be in peril.

"I think you're right, and it's our only option; at least we're holding...for now. I'm Christine by the way."

"I'm Eric, and this is Evelyn."

Eric's companion was young and obviously frightened out of her mind. She said something to him in Spanish. He answered, and she looked at me. I smiled again, this time at Evelyn. She reminded me of Tanya, and my heart went out to the young woman.

"It's okay now," I said to her. "It's all going to be fine." I was surprised at the surety in my voice. It conveyed a calmness I did not feel—not like my reaction at Haulover canal, when I thought the engine was on fire. Here we were, two boats, tangled, tossed like dice in this storm, and we were conversing like tourists at the Tiki bar.

Eric translated, and I realized that Evelyn didn't speak English.

"What's your dog's name?" I asked

"Salty," he said.

"I have one too. She's down below—not very happy right now. Her name's Kia."

"We'll have to let them get together tomorrow," he said.

"Sounds good." We talked as the boats bobbed up and down, and swung and rocked from side to side. I told them about Ed and *Nini*, and we discussed logistics and a plan for the morning.

"I'm about to make some tea. You guys want some?" I offered.

"No thanks," Erik replied. "We're gonna turn in."

After updating Ed, I poured some tea and returned to the cockpit. The wind howled, and the boat swung, stretching the anchor lines like violin strings; but for now we held tight. I sipped my tea and lit a cigarette. I began to relax then remembered that it had been a while since I last checked the bilge. I wanted off this crazy ride, but for now there was no way out.

"If you're going to sink, then sink!" I said to no one in particular. Kia raised her head and looked at me. In her eyes I saw, "shame on you—I'm here too, you know."

With a sigh I returned to the cabin and checked the bilge; the water level hadn't risen much, so I picked up the GPS and propped it on the table next to the settee. I sat and stared at the numbers.

"God, if you can hear me, please, please, don't let the numbers on the GPS change." I remembered the Bible—the one my friend Greg from Miami made me promise to buy—and rose to get it. I remembered the conversation; it was last June, just before I'd left for the Bahamas

"Greg, can you think of anything else I might need for the trip?"

"You got the Delta; you have an extra impeller, fuel filters, oil filters, batteries, spark plugs, spare fan belts...ah, yes, there's one more very important item."

"What?" I had asked, unable to imagine what I might have forgotten after weeks of preparation.

"A Bible," he said.

"A Bible? For what?"

"Do me a favor: don't argue; don't ask why; but please get a Bible and take it with you. Promise me."

I placed the Bible on the table next to the GPS and repeated my request as if it had some sort of magical power.

"God, if you can, please keep my boat exactly where it is for the rest of the night."

I watched the numbers on the GPS for a while, till my body grew heavy and it was an effort to sit up. I heaped pillows into a mound and leaned against them, struggling to maintain the vigil, but at last my eyes closed.

The sun spilled in through the portlight; I woke, picked up the Bible, and tucked it neatly onto my new bookshelf on the starboard side just forward of the mast. *Gypsy Spirit* was still bobbing furiously. Even as Eric motored his boat in circles around mine to unwind the tangled anchor line, the wind and waves sought to break free the tentative hold of my anchor. Ed directed operations from his dinghy, and soon Eric's fifty-foot steel ketch was free of my ground tackle. I'd solved the steering problem first thing in the morning when I realized that the steering cable had popped off the quadrant. Wishing all boat problems were that easily remedied, I'd replaced the cable and tightened the clamp, I'd also found and cleared the blockage that had prevented the bilge from pumping out, and now most shipboard operations were back to normal. In the light of day nothing seemed as catastrophic as it had the night before.

Ed returned to *Nini*; he would re-anchor in the cove marked *Holding Good*, then return to help me untangle my three anchors. Eric had already moved his boat to the cove and was on his way back to help.

"*Gypsy Spirit*...*Gypsy Spirit*...*Nini*—over."

"*Nini*, *Gypsy Spirit*. What's up?"

"I need help. I've got a line wrapped around the prop; my keel is already touching sand."

"Hang on, I'll tell Eric."

"Eric," I called into the wind. "Ed needs help; his anchor line is wrapped around the prop. The boat's dragging; he's almost on the beach!" Immediately Eric altered course, his dinghy airborne as it jumped from wave to wave. He reached *Nini* in seconds and dove in, disappearing from sight. He resurfaced, giving the okay signal, and I breathed a sigh of relief as *Nini* motored slowly away from the beach. Ed anchored his boat near Eric's and then the two of them returned for me. Ed pulled up the first anchor, and then unwound the second. About a half hour later, the third anchor found its place on the bow sprit.

Multiple disasters averted and miscellaneous messes sorted, it was time to unwind and let the dogs have some fun. Ed, Kia, and I motored over to Eric's boat and invited Salty to come along to the beach. Side by side at the bow, with their front paws on the pontoon, looking like figureheads, the two dogs stood proudly, noses to the wind and ears flapping in the breeze. Aside from Salty's creamy white coloring, she and Kia could have been sisters. They dug and tumbled and swam and raced along the shore. Puppy-like, with front paws and chests on the sand, rear ends raised and tails wagging, they mirrored each other's antics until, exhausted, they curled up in the cool sand of a borough they'd dug together. On that magical day, I was filled with a profound sense of thankfulness for everything. I'd had to face and overcome yet another challenge; it left me feeling so vitally alive and capable.

A Fiberglassing Goddess

Mid-November 2006

Oasis Boatyard
Saint Augustine, Florida

A fiberglassing goddess—that's what I was! Two months into the project, and at last I had a grasp of the *boat repair thing*. After the disaster of my first glassing attempt, followed by a totally disheartening week of grinding off what I'd done, I was feeling quite defeated. But then, a couple of long distance conversations with Ed on the art of laying fiberglass, and I was ready to give it another shot. I mixed up a batch of epoxy and cabosil, faired in the deeper spots, then laid three layers of glass over the hole. I went back today to check and—voila—perfection. It would be easy to prepare the surface for the next layers. What had I done differently? Twice as much epoxy to saturate the cloth, made sure the glass was translucent before applying it, wet the surface with epoxy prior to laying the cloth, squeegeed out the air using a Bondo applicator, and then, most importantly, I worked the glass in by gently dabbing with a paint brush till it lay flat and bubble free.

At last I could see the light at the end of the tunnel, not only in regard to the boat, but Ben as well. I was so close to moving back onto the boat; I would make a clean break then. Yes, I saw the light, and it was getting brighter.

Best of all, I no longer wondered why I was spending months of my life repairing the boat. It was simply something I had to do—for *me*, just like breathing. I'd never been more certain of anything in my life. I needed for the boat to be whole again. I'd come far enough to know that I wanted this, and it had nothing to do with Ed or anyone for that matter.

Regatta time in Georgetown

Chicken Harbor

March 2006 Georgetown, Bahamas

Sailboats, motorboats, mega yachts, dinghies, and houseboats, with names like *Mango* and *Papaya*—hundreds of boats, as far as the eye could see—we'd reached Elizabeth Harbor in Georgetown, home to both the Cruiser's Regatta in March and the Family Island Regatta in April. Ed had mentioned what it would be like, but nothing could have prepared me for the virtual city of boats that greeted us. As I followed him through the maze, I noted my new-found confidence in close-quarter maneuvers.

"*Gypsy Spirit*…*Gypsy Spirit*…This is *Nini*—over."

"*Nini*, this is *Gypsy Spirit*—up one," I replied, using proper radio etiquette; we had hundreds of potential listeners.

"Up one," Ed replied.

"What's up?" I inquired cheerily.

"Nothing, I was checking to see if you're okay—figured you'd be freaking out in this mess."

"Freaking out? No...this is great," I said, taking in the festive atmosphere. "I'm fine. Why...are you?" I asked, almost feeling guilty at how comfortable I was at the helm.

"No...but I knew what it would be like. Anyway, good—just stay clear of anchor lines and follow me. We'll keep going to Sand Dollar Beach."

"Sand Dollar Beach...sounds promising...don't you think, pup?" I asked Kia, who'd finally picked herself up from her depression—she'd been missing Salty—long enough to glance where I'd pointed and give a half-hearted wag. We found a clearing large enough for both boats, and a short while later, we became part of the landscape. Ed stayed behind, while Kia and I set off to explore Sand Dollar Beach. At first, caught up in my search for sand dollars, I almost missed the tiny conch-shaped, opalescent Dove shells that dotted the shoreline. There were thousands of them, and I spent a couple hours sifting through the sand, adding to what would become my extensive collection of miniature shells, sorted by genus and species. I expected it to be crowded, but we had the beach to ourselves. There was a picnic table by the water, and behind the table, winding into the shrubbery, a sandy path begged exploration. But that would have to wait for another day. I'd promised Ed I wouldn't be long; we had to make a trip into town.

We registered for the regatta, and the following day Ed's friends arrived: Lood, a fellow South African, and his friend, Richard, from the United States. That evening the four of us piled into my dinghy and motored ashore for the opening night beach party. There were several hundred cruisers in attendance.

Hot dogs and hamburgers sizzled on grills, and the sound of 60s rock rhythms filled the night air. I danced barefoot in the sand with a young captain from a neighboring boat, while Ed sulked nearby. Of course I did it all for his benefit: laughed louder, talked longer, smiled warmer, and leaned closer to the young man than I would have had Ed not be there—watching. I'd taken to gleaning this perverse pleasure whenever the opportunity presented itself; it had started in West Palm at the Tiki bar when I first noticed Ed's reaction to male attention focused in my direction.

"I just don't get it," he would say disdainfully, as if he couldn't fathom why any man would show interest in me.

"And you never will," I'd retorted.

Lood and Dick were obviously as confused by our relationship as I was; I saw it in the glances they exchanged as they tried to figure out but were too polite to ask—were we a couple? Perhaps they asked Ed, at night when it was just the guys. It might have been my imagination, but I felt as though Lood, who was like a father to Ed, especially wanted us to be together and was upset with my flirtations at the beach party.

The days unfurled in a flurry of activity, and I enjoyed the security of knowing that at least for a while there would be no obstacles to surmount, no storms, and no mechanical malfunctions. I felt as though I'd been holding my breath since we'd left the States, and at last I was able to exhale and relax as Georgetown and this harbor became home. No matter that Ed said "don't get too comfortable"—comfortable is exactly what I got. Kia and I hiked and explored the meandering paths that took us from the anchorage, through the shrubbery, up the rocky slopes overlooking the Atlantic, and down to the beach.

We surfed the waves and roamed the sandy shore. Long hours of sun and salt lightened my hair to a soft gold; my tan deepened to a warm cocoa brown, and the hours spent swimming, climbing, and running toned and strengthened my body and my soul.

We played volleyball behind Chat 'n' Chill's Restaurant and ate freshly made conch salad on the beach. Cruisers gathered to play bridge or take a watercolor or yoga class; there was a beach school for the children and church on Sundays. There were games and contests daily. We signed up for the races and attended a captain's meeting, where it became clear that the "just for fun" races weren't necessarily just for fun. On race day we adopted a unique strategy and did a bit of fishing on our particularly long tack. During the closing ceremony, the crew of *Gypsy Spirit* proudly accepted the Turtle Award for having achieved last place in the race. And so the days passed; Lood and Dick left for home, and Tanya arrived to spend her spring break with me.

At last my daughter was with me, and for the next week, she'd get to experience the thrill of life aboard ship in the islands. It wasn't months, like we planned, but she was here, and that's all that mattered. I would show her the best of cruising, and as far as I was concerned, deserted beaches were as good as it got. So on her first morning, after coffee, Tanya, Kia, and I loaded into the dinghy and headed over to Sand Dollar Beach.

"Oh my god, Mom, look at all these shells," she said, discovering as I had the myriad of Dove shells littering the sand.

"Those are nothing; wait till you see where we're going. Come on," I said and took off at a slow jog up the sandy path into the woods. Tanya bounded in and raced off ahead of me up the hill and was in the lead until Kia darted past us both. I picked up the pace, and after about five minutes the two of us reached the top, out of breath and laughing.

"Where does that path go?" she asked, pointing to the trail that snaked off to our right.

"Along the top of the cliff—it's beautiful. We'll go that way later and take some pictures, but let's go to the beach now. See you there," I called and loped off down the narrow path.

"Hey!"

By the time we reached the bottom, Kia was already in the water; we raced in after her and threw ourselves into the surf. We spent that day on the beach; bodysurfing, collecting shells, taking pictures, talking, and laughing. It had been so long since we'd had time alone, and now here we were, together in paradise.

After a while the sun got to be too much for Kia, so we built a lean-to out of bamboo and bits of wreckage that we found on the beach. We thatched the roof with palm fronds and hung our sarongs to create a wall; then the three of us slipped into the shelter we'd created.

"This is the life—don't you think?" I asked.

"Yeah, it's pretty cool."

"You know, on one hand I'm actually glad that you flew here and missed some of the adventure." I told Tanya about the night at Leaf Cay and about Evelyn and how frightened she had been. "I would have hated to put you through that. At least now you get to enjoy all the good stuff, with no worries."

"I wouldn't have worried, Mom. I trust you."

I was touched by her faith in me, but it raised a question that I'd been mulling over for some time and I wanted Tanya's opinion. Our departure date was fast approaching. "What do you think about me not going any further with Ed?"

"What do you mean?"

"I'm kind of thinking about staying here for a while, then heading back, the way we came."

"Why?"

"I don't know. I have this really bad feeling. Ed says it's because we stayed here too long—he says it happens to everyone…but I don't know. What do you think?"

"You have to do what feels right."

"Big help, thanks." But I knew she was right—it had to be my decision and mine alone. "Come on, let's go swimming. I'm getting hot."

Although we began each day of her short visit on our beach, afternoons found us exploring Georgetown or snorkeling with Ed in search of conch for dinner.

One night we went with Ed to a *rake 'n' scrape* and watched people dancing to the rhythm of the goombay drum. This style of music had its roots in Africa but evolved in the Bahamas. The name came from the scraping sound created by running a knife blade against the teeth of the carpenter saw.

Most evenings however, we spent quietly enjoying the water and the sights and sounds of the harbor from the cockpit of my boat. We sat talking, the three of us, late into each evening, and I marveled at the glow created by hundreds of anchor-lights glittering like stars in the night sky. I wished I could stop time and be given at least a month to savor with my daughter, but it seemed that no sooner had she arrived, it was time to say goodbye. I hugged her and wished her a safe journey home. I promised to call as soon as possible, and then she was gone. I still wasn't sure what to do, and we were supposed to leave Georgetown in a couple of days.

I woke clutching the bottle of coconut rum I'd won the previous night in a limbo contest at the Pirate Bob party. I smiled; *yes*, I still had it after all these years; I could limbo with the best of them. But then I turned to get up and remembered the other "prize" earned from my exertions—a pulled thigh muscle; I shimmied over to edge of the bunk and gingerly rose to my feet; I could barely stand. Dizzy and nursing a blinding headache, I went through the motions of getting ready, but my heart wasn't in it. I was not prepared to leave the safety of the harbor for the unknown, but as planned we weighed anchor, and I led the way to Conch Cay Cut. About halfway through, I was gripped by a paralyzing sense that something really bad was going to happen. The seas were still kicked up from a passing cold front, and I suppose that didn't help calm my nerves.

"*Nini…Nini…Gypsy Spirit*— over," I called into the receiver.

"*Gypsy Spirit*, this is *Nini*—go up one."

"Up one."

"*Nini?*"

"Ya, what's up?"

"I'm turning around. I don't feel good about this," I said.

"You can't turn around; you're in the cut—you're committed."

"I can, and I'm going to," I responded, remembering my promise to myself not to head out anymore when things didn't feel right. I had to make my own decisions.

"Listen...you turn back, you're going back alone."

"Fine!" I tossed receiver.

"*Gypsy Spirit...Gypsy Spirit...Nini*—over..."

"*Gypsy Spirit...Gypsy Spirit...Nini*—over..."

I had nothing to say. If he went on without me, so be it.

My sense of foreboding lifted exponentially with each turn of the propeller. I headed in, past the spot where we were anchored last night, past all the other boats. I traveled well over a mile before I ventured a look back toward the cut. Ed had also turned around. I slowed my boat to an idle and waited till he caught up with me. He passed without looking in my direction. I followed him to Fowl Cay and anchored.

"*Gypsy Spirit*, this is *Nini*—over."

"*Nini*, this is *Gypsy Spirit*."

"Would you mind coming over. I'd like to speak with you." His dinghy was stored on deck; it was easier to launch mine from the davits.

He sounded really calm, deceptively calm, and I wasn't sure what to expect. "Sure, I'll be over in a few," I answered in a similarly lighthearted tone. Ten minutes later, after gathering everything he'd lent me into a box, I pulled up next to his boat.

"What's all this?" he asked, pointing to the container sitting on the floor of the dinghy, filled to the brim with: books, tools, binoculars, sunglasses, and other odds and ends.

"Your stuff," I answered.

"I know that. But why are you giving it to me?" he asked.

"Because I'm not going on."

If he had been planning some kind of lecture, it went by the wayside, and he reached down to take the container from me. "Why? What's happened all of the sudden?"

"Ed, it's not all of the sudden. You haven't been listening to me. I have a really bad feeling about this. I don't know why. It doesn't make any sense, but I get sick at the thought of heading on."

"We've been here too long, that's all. You've gotten complacent," he said. "Do you know what they call this place?"

I shook my head.

"Chicken Harbor. Do you want to know why?" He didn't wait for my response, "Because people make it this far, stay too long, and then they get scared. They turn around and head back."

"No, this is different," I countered.

"What's going to happen to you if you don't come with me? How are you going to get home?" he asked.

"I don't know, and right now I don't care. I'll figure it out when I'm ready. I'll probably just sail back the way we came."

"You're not being rational," he said.

"I've made up my mind."

"Okay, fine. I give up." He shrugged. "I'll get your stuff," he said and ducked down into the cabin, reappearing several minutes later with a couple of books and movies. As he handed me my stuff, he said, "Do me a favor."

"What?"

"When you go back to your boat, make a list of pros and cons: reasons to quit, reasons to continue…with me. Would you do that, please? Then come back and talk to me, one more time."

Ed greeted me with a big smile when I returned hours later. "I was beginning to think you weren't coming back," he said, taking the line from my hand as I boarded.

"The list took longer than I thought…"

Ed raised an eyebrow.

"And I guess I fell asleep for a bit."

"A bit—more like three hours, you heartless wench. How could you possibly sleep when I…"

Ignoring his teasing, I pulled a folded sheet from my pocket and handed it to him.

"Hmm…interesting," he said after studying the list for a few moments.

"What?"

"You have *so many unknowns* listed as both a pro and a con."

"Yeah."

"Why?" he asked.

"Because it is both."

"Really?"

"On the one hand, I'll never know what wonderful things might have been, what amazing experiences I'll miss. But, then again, I won't have to worry about what bad things might happen anymore, either."

"So this is it—final decision?"

"Ed, I'm really sorry. I can't explain it, but I just can't go on."

"I'm sorry, too—sorry that I got you into this."

"Don't say that. There's nothing for you to be sorry about. I wouldn't change a single moment." *Except maybe I would have liked to have had the courage to tell you how I feel instead of playing silly games.*

We were quiet for a time, then Ed spoke. "I'm not leaving till at least six-thirty…if you change your mind…I'll wait for you."

"Okay. I've got to go. Give me a hug goodbye."

"I'll hug you," he said, awkwardly putting his arms around me, "but no goodbyes."

Resisting momentarily the urge to crawl into bed and hide, I pulled the list from my pocket and read…

Pros

- *major sense of accomplishment*
- *2 more months of adventure*
- *visit more islands and the Dominican Republic*
- *face and overcome fear*
- *feel really sad and empty when I imagine morning arriving and I realize it's over*
- *i remember how awesome it felt on the ocean when things were good*
- *once in a lifetime opportunity*
- *i know I'll regret it forever if I don't go*
- *so many unknowns. . .*

The list was incomplete, and I knew it. I'd omitted one very important reason to continue—Ed. I continued reading…

Cons

- *get sick to my stomach every time I think of heading out.*
- *what if something worse than Leaf Cay happens*
- *relieved when I think of not going on*
- *elephants on the horizon*
- *feel trapped*
- *what if we get caught in a blow*
- *what if the weather changes faster than expected*
- *I know now what it's like to feel trapped and scared for hours*
- *what if I can't rise to the occasion when it's called for*
- *so many unknowns. . .*

"I made the right decision," I said as my eyes lingered on one particular line. *I know now what it's like to feel trapped and scared for hours.* The emotions I'd experienced on that tumultuous night at Leaf Cay were still fresh, and I never ever wanted to feel that way again. "I just can't do it." I was not the type of person to "get back up on the horse." I crumpled the list and tossed it in the trash.

Kia sighed and stretched out on the settee, settling in, oblivious to the melee raging in my mind.

"Good idea; time for bed," I announced and climbed into my berth. I closed my eyes, forced them to remain shut even though they burned to open. For a while I lay on my stomach, then rolled onto my back, then onto my side: the hours passed, but try as I might, I couldn't sleep—I was afraid I'd wake and find Ed gone. I rose from the tangled mess of bed sheets and retrieved the list, flattened it with my fingers, then read it once again.

"Kia, if something bad is gonna happen, it could happen anytime anywhere. Something bad could happen right here."

Kia looked up from the settee.

"I can't live my life in fear. Otherwise I might as well lock myself inside the house and never go out again."

Kia cocked her head.

"Am I going to let fear rule my life?"

Kia sat up expectantly and looked toward the companionway.

"Come on, pup, we're going to finish this trip. We'll sail this boat to the Dominican Republic, and nothing's going to stop us. Come on. Let's go ashore. We have to leave in two hours."Ed called the moment we returned from the beach.

"How long till you're ready?" he asked.

"About a half hour—how did you know?"

"I didn't; I just hoped," he answered.

We traveled twenty-four gloriously uneventful nautical miles to Cape Santa Maria on Long Island and anchored before sunset. That night, sitting on the beach, cocktails in hand, we toasted, and I thanked Ed for not giving up on me. Everything was perfect; so what that it had taken eleven hours to cover twenty-four miles. It felt so good to be there in that moment. That night before I fell asleep, I looked up at the shimmering expanse blanketing the sky and prayed.

"God, please watch over us; and by the way…in case I've forgotten, I just want to say…thank you."

Imagine looking out and whichever way you turn—water: not a sliver of land, not another boat in sight. I didn't have to imagine; we were alone, Kia and I and *Gypsy Spirit*, sailing along at a very admirable six knots across an ocean that was over a mile deep. I preferred not to dwell on the last fact, even though I knew we could just as easily sink in fifty feet of water. We'd left Ed behind soon after dawn on the second day of our one-hundred-fifty-mile trek from Long Island to West Plana Cay—the longest leg so far. We were supposed to be traveling together, but as soon as I'd seen the clouds building, billowing toward the sky, I knew he would call and tell me to go on alone.

"I don't want to," I'd argued. "We should stay together."

"You see the clouds," he said. "It's going to get bad, and I won't be able to help you. I'll be dealing with my own shit."

"But I can—"

"Don't—I need to know that you're safely anchored. Besides, I can't make it to the anchorage before dark. You need to check it out and find a safe place for me to anchor."

And that was that. I'd looked back from time to time, but once Ed's mast had disappeared into the horizon, I noticed how peaceful, how really nice it was, not having to worry about another boat. I passed the time looking at shapes in the thickening clouds. A gigantic poodle emerged, and the Michelin man held a unicorn in his hand. With each hour the clouds grew like heads of cauliflower bursting upwards, and thunderheads formed. Finally in the distance, with the sun still peeking out every now and then from behind the clouds, I made out the faintest bit of land. An hour later I was anchored safely in twelve feet of water, about a quarter mile off the beach at West Plana Cay.

I took Kia ashore, and we spent the remaining part of the day stretching our legs on the deserted little island. It was an unimaginable thrill to know that we were the solitary inhabitants of this tiny bit of land. Ed arrived just before sunset, and after settling in he came over for a visit.

We rose early the next morning and walked the perimeter of the island; I followed behind, stopping here and there to pluck a shell or piece of coral from the sand. Ed fished, and that night we dined on grouper and watched the sun set by an island where the only footprints in the sand were ours. The boat bobbed gently upon water so clear I watched a starfish walk along the ocean floor. Short of wishing I could share this moment with my dad and Tanya, I couldn't imagine anything more perfect. I was filled with an indescribable, wordless sense of contentment.

"You know, I've always dreamt of being shipwrecked on a deserted island. I think it would be so cool," I said, breaking the silence as we sat just before sunset, hoping to catch a glimpse of the Green Flash.

Ed gave me one of his "duh" looks then turned back toward the setting sun.

"Really," I insisted. "I think it would be exciting. Can you imagine…building a shelter, foraging for food, collecting water…"

"No, it wouldn't be exciting, and I don't want to imagine," Ed interrupted. "What makes you think there will be fresh water?"

"I'd drink coconut milk," I answered, surprised by his vehemence.

"Maybe…if there happened to be coconut palms on your island…you don't get to choose where you're shipwrecked, and you won't have time to gather tools and a survival kit, not to mention food for the hound. You better pray that it never happens. This isn't a game, you know."

"Whoa, calm down. I know; it's just a fantasy, that's all. But if it did happen, I'd do just fine."

"Oh, you think so? *Fine*? Okay, you have two minutes—grab whatever you can and then I'm taking you ashore. You are being shipwrecked."

I laughed.

"You're wasting time; I'm not kidding," he said.

I had to admit, a small part of me, actually a big part of me, was thrilled, but—and it was a very big *but*…

"Very funny, but it won't work."

"What won't work?" Ed asked then looked at the clock. "Fifty-five seconds…May I suggest: food and water for the hound and a flashlight. It will be dark soon."

"Ed, cut it out. I am not going anywhere."

"No?"

"No. It's not exactly what I had in mind; this island is completely barren: there's no water, no trees, no coconuts, nothing to build with…It wouldn't be any fun."

"*What?*" he asked incredulously. "Being shipwrecked wouldn't be any fun?"

"You know what I mean."

"Yes, I know. Be very careful what you wish for—that's *all* I'm saying. Damn, woman, you made me miss the Green Flash," he said.

"Didn't happen; I was watching."

The perfection of yesterday was long forgotten as I sailed along wondering what I was doing following a cranky lunatic through the Caribbean. We'd departed West Plana early, intending to cover the twenty-eight miles to Mayaguana in about six hours. Eight hours later and with thirteen miles still to go, I tried hailing Ed.

"*Nini*...*Nini*...This is *Gypsy Spirit*—over." No response. I tried again and then decided to sail up closer.

"*Nini*...*Nini*...This is *Gypsy Spirit*—over." After two more attempts, he answered.

"*Gypsy Spirit*, what do you want?"

"Nothing—I thought maybe something was wrong. I was just checking," I answered, stunned by his sharp response.

"And if it was, what were you going to do?"

"I was going to help."

"Really," he replied sarcastically, "and what—swim over and sort me out? Listen, I can't deal with this right now. Would you please head on and stop lurking around behind me?"

Lurking? Did he just say I was *lurking*? It had been a very long day and my nerves were raw.

"Fine. See you. Bye." And that was it. I sailed away, leaving Ed behind—again. Finally after twelve hours and still fuming, I anchored in Start Bay, Mayaguana. Ed was nowhere in sight as I brought the dinghy around and held it in place for Kia to jump down. I was angry enough that I barely noticed the huge swells banging and bobbing the dinghy up and down against the hull. Kia noticed and hesitated, timing her leap with the moment a wave lifted the dinghy to the deck.

"What did I do to him?" I asked Kia as we walked along the beach. She paused then promptly returned her attention to a small bubbling hole in the sand.

"I was only trying to find out if he was having engine problems...I could have helped...if he let me." He obviously didn't think I was capable and that hurt. We finished exploring in silence, and for the first time since embarking on our journey, I returned to the dinghy empty-handed: no shells, no bits of coral, no lucky beans, no coconuts, and no gourds.

The dinghy bounced and spluttered its way back to the boat.

"Great—another roly-poly anchorage from hell. We're in for quite the carnival ride tonight, Kia."

I strolled along the beach, dragging my heels in the sand—nature's pedicure. The sun shone bright and warm, and this morning walk was a welcome though brief respite from the bouncing and rolling. I wondered for the thousandth time why we had to race through the Bahamas. As far as I was concerned, this was the best part of the trip; when would I get to walk the shores of a deserted island again? I knew Ed had been through this island chain countless times, and he was really eager to get to the Dominican Republic. We'd be there in a few days, and I hoped it would be all he'd described.

"Come on, Kia. We better get going." We motored over to Ed's boat but kept the visit short, due in part to yesterday's altercation, but more so to the large swells, which were increasing in size by the minute. Even I knew when it was time to haul anchor, and the time was now, but it was quite the trick getting Kia aboard. With one hand I held the dinghy against the side of the boat; with the other I held Kia's scruff. All the while the dinghy was rising and falling and dipping and dancing.

We had planned to go to Abraham Bay but turned back en route after being warned by another boat of rough seas in the bay. We sailed north past Betsy Bay to Northwest Point where we found a clear patch of sand to anchor and much calmer seas.

Ed's mood had definitely improved, and by the time we stepped ashore, it was as though nothing had happened. Northwest Point, Mayaguana, was a beachcombing scavenger's paradise, and I was in heaven. Every genus and species in my Caribbean shell book seemed to be represented on these shores: limpets and coquina, bubble shells and olives, top shells and turbans, conchs and cones, trivia shells and flamingo tongues, star shells and cowries, nerites and chitons, sea urchins and sand dollars, lucky beans, hamburger beans, coral and coconuts, gourds and bamboo—you name it, it was here. Kia explored the tidal pools while Ed walked the strandline and sorted through seaweed and driftwood in search of the perfect piece of bamboo.

"Would you like me to make you an ashtray like mine?" Ed asked.

"Sure, I'd love one," I said, remembering the stout round bamboo ashtray with palm trees carved into the side. My heart warmed at the thought of him making something for me, and a smile played about my lips for the entire ride back to the boat. Ed looked at me quizzically but said nothing.

"I need a hacksaw, a drill, some sandpaper…oh, and a chisel if you've got one," Ed said.

"Coming right up," I replied and gathered the tools. "I'm going to make us some lunch while you're doing that."

"Sounds good," Ed said.

Sometime later I closed the oven door and looked up from the companionway; Ed was busy cutting and sanding; Kia dozed, nose twitching from time to time, in the midafternoon sun.

"Smells good. What's cooking?" Ed asked.

"Cheese and garlic biscuits," I replied. It had been days since we'd had any kind of bread, and these warm biscuits would be delicious, dripping with melted butter and smothered in raspberry jam. "They'll be done in a minute."

"Good. I will too." Ed said proudly and handed me the first of two ashtrays that he'd made. "You can't break these ones."

I laughed. "They're beautiful, Ed. Thank you."

"They need some carvings or something," he said, handing me the second one, "but I'll leave that to you."

"I like them just the way they are," I said and ducked below to get the biscuits. Ed saw me put another tray in the oven.

"What was that?" he asked.

"Oh, I made chocolate cake too."

"Brave woman—you remember what happened the last time you made sweets," he warned.

"That's not funny," I said, remembering Leaf Cay and the fudge incident.

We ate in companionable silence, savoring the biscuits and the moment, thankful for the peaceful anchorage and lovely day, blissfully unaware that our lives were about to undergo a dramatic change.

The Ship's Log

December 2006

Oasis Boatyard
Saint Augustine, Florida

Never failed—as soon as I'd mastered one technique, it was time to start from the beginning with something new. I'd finished most of the grinding and glassing and had begun fairing in the hull, bow, and deck. Done properly, the damage and repairs would be invisible. The process involved applying epoxy mixed with compounds of varying density then sanding between each layer, until at last, a mirror finish was achieved. The problem was that I'd applied layer after layer, and no matter how much I shaped and sanded, the damage was clearly visible. I was more than a week behind schedule and about to head north for the holidays. I hired the boatyard to drop the rudder and complete the interior grinding. Hopefully they'd get it done while I was in Boston, then when I returned, I'd glass in the tabs and bulkheads and move back aboard. It would be a new year and a new life.

I pulled out my ship's log to record some repairs and a couple of purchases. I turned the book over in my hand, appreciating not for the first time the beauty of the jacket and the gilded pages, crafted to look like an old-time journal. Despite looking worn and beaten, the pages stained here and there when a rogue wave emptied the contents of my coffee mug, it was no less beautiful. Part ship's log, part journal, the book had evolved into a diary of the restoration. In it I recorded daily triumphs and disasters as well as every penny that went into the project—so far I was on budget. As the months passed, I'd become intimately familiar with my boat—every nut and bolt of her, counted and sized—was recorded in the journal for future reference. I rifled the pages and inhaled the scent of salt air, laced with diesel fuel and engine oil. The aromas mingled into memories; the book fell open…

Sunday, April 9

One hundred seventy miles to South Caicos, by far the longest leg of our journey, and I am dreading it. We are going to sail around the northwest tip of Mayaguana then run along the top of the island and over the Turks and Caicos, rather than across the bank like most. After that we'll be in the home stretch, with the Dominican Republic about a day away. Ed said we'd be sailing in the lee for a while and if all goes well we'll arrive in South Caicos tomorrow night. When I do the math, it doesn't quite work out like that.

Monday, April 10 0836 hours

What can I say—gray, dismal, drizzly. I am down to my last eight cigarettes. I don't want to think how much farther we have to go. A seagull rode on the boat with me last night for a few hours. There really isn't much more to say. I feel like we're not making any progress. We still haven't passed the top of Mayaguana. I'm really worried about Kia. She refuses to pee and I don't want her to get a urinary tract infection. Also I think the engine is leaking diesel; the smell is so strong. I have to check it out.

1315 hours

Well, we are still en route to the Turks and Caicos via the north pole! There's definitely a leak in the fuel system. I shut the engine off. I'm concerned about fuel consumption.

1758 hours

Okay, I'm in a much better mood now. I've been sailing since the engine went off, and it's nice—really nice. A pod of dolphins is swimming with me, surfacing, diving. Ed and I talked. I told him I was having a hard time going so slow, and he suggested I go on ahead, so I'm off. I have to keep bearing east as much as possible. God, it's nice not having to watch out for his boat: nothing but ocean and sky. I'm looking forward to my solitary adventure. Tom Petty is in the CD player. My favorite song is playing.

"you belong among the wildflowers,
you belong in a boat out at sea,
you belong with your love on your own,
you belong somewhere you feel free"

2106 hours

I need to maintain a course of 130 degrees so I put the engine back on. I've got to get some rest. I'm going to set my phone alarm for fifteen minutes, close my eyes, and force myself to relax.

Tuesday, April 11 0726hours

I hope I make it to South Caicos today. I have to call and wish my dad and Tanya a happy birthday. I am still plodding along on my southeasterly trek. Ideally I need to hold a course between 120 and 140 degrees, but right now, for comfort and speed, I am running between 150 and 170 degrees. I won't clear the whole of the bank this way, but I should be able to do my easting in a bit. There's no sign of Ed. The diesel smell is worse. Tightening the nut didn't solve the problem.

1130 hours

All hell has broken loose. The fuel system is down. I can't start the engine; there is air in the lines; and I'm almost out of diesel. I was hit by a rogue wave, and the computer fell below and broke. I no longer have charts; the only thing I have is a waypoint for the reefs at the eastern tip of East Caicos and the knowledge that from there I should be on a heading of 225 degrees for approximately fifteen miles. There are thunderheads everywhere. I have reefed in anticipation of squalls. Also the wind speed monitor and the depth sounder have chosen to join the list of defunct equipment.

1800 hours

The anemometer came back sometime during the storm. Oh, yeah, did I forget to mention that bit. Not sure exactly when it started—must have been about noon—I've basically been pummeled for six hours. The boat was literally picked up and tossed on its side maybe twenty times—tough little boat. Most of the sky seems to be clearing except the direction I'm heading in. When the storm began, I had twenty-three miles to go to get to my one and only waypoint. I now have fourteen. I was trying to find a way to handle the storm comfortably and managed to balance my sails and hold a course without the autopilot. I can't use the autopilot anymore. I don't want to run the batteries down since I have no way to charge them without the engine, and I can't risk losing the VHF and bilge pump—not to mention lights. I wish Ed would magically appear.

1918 hrs

Finally managed to tack. The seas are still up, and the wind has lightened, so I had a hard time getting up enough speed to make it over the eight to ten foot swells. I kept stalling out and falling back on the same course, but I had to tack—I was making too much leeway toward the reefs. If I hadn't changed course soon, we'd wreck. I remembered what Ed said about being careful of what you wish for. . .Maybe this was my fault. Anyway, I realized that I'd been trying to force the boat; I was rushing things. So I let the boat build speed;

I took my time, then climbed the wave on an angle, tacked at the crest, and caught the wind as we rode down the back side.

Currently I'm on a heading of 320 degrees. I am sort of hove to, traveling at about one and a half knots. I want to get away from the reefs, but with the whole night ahead, I don't want to get too far out. The wind has picked up again, but the boat is lying comfortably. I'm already a mile further away from the reefs—what a relief.

I have given up hope of reaching land tonight. Perhaps if I hadn't lost my computer and if my depth sounder were still working and I could start my engine and navigate the reefs in the dark, I'd be tucked into an anchorage right now.

Happy Birthday, Tanya; Happy Birthday, Dad; I'll be there next year—I promise.

I closed the book and sighed. If only I'd known or had heeded the voices. I would have seen…In the distance, a two-hundred-sixty-foot container ship en route to West Palm coursed through the rough sea. The vessel had picked up speed since the storm subsided. At eighteen knots and on its present course, it would soon make up for lost time. The ship carried a crew of eight men plus the captain. Most of the men were resting, preparing for a routine night's passage. The captain and engineer were on the bridge. The ship's radar scanned the horizon. A blip appeared on the monitor, and the engineer notified the captain. They studied the image, and then disregarded what they saw as static caused by the storm. In a moment I would disappear from radar. My sailboat would be hidden by a blind spot.

Enjoying the beauty…blissfully unaware

Collision At Sea

April 2006 North of the Turks and Caicos Islands

I was seated on the portside settee getting ready to calculate my current position and make some notes in the ship's log. It was deceptively calm below deck—so far from the turbulent sea and wind. But I couldn't quite relax; there was a strange nagging voice in my head: "scan the horizon, scan the horizon," it repeated. I fought the urge to return to deck and check for ships yet again. It had only been eight minutes since my last round. I forced myself to sit back. I lifted my legs and placed them on the table, then rested the log book against my knees and began drawing a circle. Within the circle, I drew an arrow to indicate our current course and then a line for wind direction.

Without warning—CRASH—the loudest, jarring, explosive sound ripped through the cabin, tearing into the core of my vessel: splintering wood, crunching metal. I couldn't breathe—acrid stench. BANGING—GRINDING—my boat tearing apart…

Kia's terrified yowls...the starboard paneling caving in like a dollhouse.

And I was frozen, transfixed, staring at the spot where the sea would no doubt come roaring in...I waited...held my breath, afraid to exhale...I waited and waited for what seemed like forever, but somehow the hull kept the angry sea at bay. I scrambled to the companionway, looked up, and watched in horror as the monster of a ship scraped and ground its way along my hull. I craned my neck back, looked up, and read the name towering atop the freighter—*Mystic Gem*.

I surveyed the wreckage: the starboard woodwork and cabinetry had caved in; above deck, the starboard spreader was gone and the shroud severed. The clock read 2035 hours. I grabbed the VHF transmitter, hoping to get a message out before we were out of range.

"*Mystic Gem*... *Mystic Gem*... This is the sailing vessel *Gypsy Spirit*—over."

Nothing.

"*Mystic Gem*... *Mystic Gem*... This is the sailing vessel *Gypsy Spirit*—you've hit me!—over."

Nothing.

I watched the monster of a ship grow smaller; soon it would be gone. The severed end of the shroud swung, clanging against the mast where the spreader had been. I listened to Kia's pitiful howls, wondering how long till the rig failed, how long till the crack in the hull opened to the waiting sea.

"*Mystic Gem*...*Mystic Gem*...This is the sailing vessel *Gypsy Spirit*—can you hear me?"

Turn around...please don't leave.

The ship's lights began to fade; the transmitter slipped from my fingers. It was time to make a plan. We had an hour, maybe less, till…

"*Gypsy Spirit*…*Gypsy Spirit*…This is the captain of M/V *Mystic Gem.*" I couldn't believe my ears. I glanced at the clock: 2040 hours. Had it only been five minutes? I reached down and snatched the transmitter from where it had landed.

"*Gypsy Spirit*…*Gypsy Spirit*…This is M/V *Mystic Gem*—over," the voice repeated.

"Yes, Captain, this is *Gypsy Spirit.*"

"How many passengers do you have on board?"

"Two—myself and my dog."

"Any injuries?"

"No."

"Are you taking on water?"

"Yes, but the bilge pump seems to be keeping up. My rigging's damaged. I don't know how long the mast will stand."

"We are coming about, but it will take a while for us to turn, and before we get there, you need to take your sails down. Can you go below and check the condition of the leak?"

I lifted the settee cushions to examine the damage. Three cracks snaked along the hull and extended below the waterline. They were weeping a steady stream into the boat. I could hear the comforting whir of the bilge pump as it fought to keep the boat from sinking. I remembered the night at Leaf Cay, when the bilge pump stopped pumping, and a shudder ran down my spine. Would we stay afloat? I checked the bilge; the water level had not risen.

"Captain, are you there?" I called into the receiver.

"Yes...Go ahead."

"There are three cracks in the hull, but I think the bilge pump is keeping up. I'm going to wait to bring the sails down; they're helping to keep the boat steady. But I'll be ready when you get here."

"Roger that—don't turn your radio off."

I tried to coax Kia from the cabin. My fifty-pound pup fought and struggled to remain huddled in the chaotic mass of pillows and jumbled blankets. Grabbing hold of the strap on the back of her life jacket, I dragged her into the main cabin then began gathering essentials: boat papers, passport, wallet, insurance documents.

Approximately thirty minutes later, with the ship fast approaching, I furled the jib, dropped the main, secured the halyards, and prayed for the best. I lifted and shoved Kia onto her ramp and up to the cockpit. She tried to jump back down; I tied her to the steering pedestal.

The ship loomed to starboard; the crew was gathered at the rail, peering down at me, through the darkness, with the same curiosity with which I stared up at them. We were close enough for me to hear their voices; they were speaking, but not in English. One man coiled a length of line and gestured for me to move to the bow. Without the steadying effect of sails, the boat rolled wildly, but somehow the mast stood, and I made my way forward. I clung to the lower shroud as the boat reared and dove. I waited and watched as the man tossed the line into the darkness. I couldn't see a thing, but I raised my arm...ready... waiting...a moment, forever...and then... inconceivably, I felt a sharp pinch as the very end of the line landed directly in my outstretched palm. I closed my fingers quickly and tightly around the monkey's fist, then made to secure the line to a bow cleat. I scrambled along the deck to the stern, opened the lazarette, retrieved as long a line as I could find, attached one end to a stern cleat, and tossed the line as hard as I could, up UP *it rose* toward the crew on *Mystic Gem*. I'd swear it was carried by an angel and placed in the sailor's hand—my aim could not have been that true on such a dark and stormy night.

Moments later, *Gypsy Spirit* was brought alongside the massive freighter, and a new worry emerged. Although the freighter sat well in the rough sea, my boat was lifting and smashing into *Mystic Gem*'s hull, and I didn't know how much more *Gypsy Spirit* could withstand. A rope ladder appeared, tumbling down from above, and a voice called out.

"You come now."

"No, wait," I said, gesturing to Kia.

"Quickly, quickly," he said. "You come."

"No! My dog! Please…lower a rope!"

"Dog bite! No dog!" he called back.

"The dog won't bite! You have to take my dog! Please!" I yelled back.

There was no reply. Two men argued; one gestured wildly and shook his head. I waited, terrified but resolute. I had one hand on the strap of Kia's life jacket, one on the wheel. Leaving without her was not an option, and if the men wouldn't take her, I'd have to cut loose soon. The boat could not take much more of this punishment. My mind worked fast, weighing the options, while I prayed: please take the dog…please take the dog. As if in answer, a rope spiraled to the deck.

"Quickly, bring dog!"

I tied the line to Kia's life jacket and pulled her from the cockpit; she was hoisted, howling, from the deck. She swung like a pendulum in a wide arc, dangling from the end of the line as I watched helplessly, listening to her terrified cries. I couldn't move—couldn't breathe. What if she fell? What if they let go? Everything moved in slow motion. Slowly…slowly…painstakingly slowly, she was lifted, and then at last, I saw hands; they grabbed and pulled her over the rail. I breathed—she was safely aboard.

My turn—one last glance—I was thankful to be getting off but feeling a certain sense of guilt. I shook my head, breathed deep, and moved toward the ladder—the rungs were just out of reach—but then in the next instant, a wave lifted my boat high enough for me to reach the ladder. I grabbed hold as the deck fell out from beneath me and the stanchions where I'd just been standing were crushed flat against the cabin side. I pulled my body up and managed to get my feet onto the bottom rung. I struggled upwards—the men called out in encouragement. And then I was lifted, like a gaffed fish, they hauled me over the rail and onto the deck.

The next wave lifted, wrenching *Gypsy Spirit* roughly, taking down the top half of the mast, and tearing the bowsprit from the deck. My boat swung freely, attached only at the stern. I gripped the rail on the deck of the container ship and strained forward trying to see. I would most certainly lose my boat.

A blanket was draped over my shoulders, and I was being pulled away from the rail.

"Please, you come now. We take care of boat," a voice said.

"But…"

"You come now. Get warm. Come...come..." a sailor urged smiling warmly as he ushered me inside. Dry clothes appeared and flip flops, which I accepted gratefully, having been rescued barefoot, shivering, and wearing a bathing suit.

Warm and dry for the first time in almost ten hours, and having been assured that my boat was finally safely in tow, I sat at a long table in the galley surrounded by six curious smiling faces. There was some sort of debate going on, and from what the crew related in broken English, it seemed the ship's doctor was intent on medicating me, while the cook felt that a good meal would cure whatever ailed me.

"Medicine—I give you medicine...You sleep," the doctor said.

"No medicine, thank you."

"Yes, you take medicine. You sleep—feel better," he urged.

"Really, I don't need medicine." I smiled.

The doctor looked rather frustrated and said, "Medicine good—you take—feel better."

"Really, I am fine, and I don't want any medicine. But, thank you anyway."

"Okay." He shrugged. Obviously disappointed, he stepped back.

Now it was the cook's turn. Having watched the doctor fail, he decided to feed me into a stupor.

"You eat now...dinner—fry eggs, sandwich, maybe coffee...you like coffee, tea?"

"I would love a cup of coffee, thank you so much."

The cook smiled; he'd succeeded where the doctor had failed.

They must have thought that I'd been lost at sea for ages. They had no way of knowing that I'd been gorging on chocolate cake less than two hours ago, but I was definitely craving a cigarette. The tea leaves and leftover tobacco that I'd rolled in West Marine catalog pages just weren't the same. One of the crew members smoked and gave me his only pack, which we shared.

The men overcame their initial uncertainty about Kia and brought her blankets for a bed, water, and all the Spam she could eat. Gary, the sailor who'd given me the clothes and flip flops and who spoke the most English, teased me.

"Be careful! Cook—he cook dog," he said, smiling then translated for the cook, who looked taken aback.

"No...no cook. Good dog," the cook assured me and shook his head.

"Excuse me, the captain asked me to invite you to the bridge," said the engineer, appearing suddenly at the galley entrance.

I excused myself and rose to follow the engineer up the stairs. The captain was seated, looking at a computer terminal, but he turned at the sound of our footsteps. He smiled.

"Come in; have a seat." He motioned to a chair near him.

"Thank you," I said.

"The crew just notified me that your boat is safely in tow. We almost lost a man overboard, trying to save your boat..."

"Oh my god...is he okay?" I couldn't bear it if someone was hurt—or worse.

"Yes, yes...Everything is all right now. Tell me, are you okay? Are you hurt? Those bruises on your leg?" he asked, pointing to the purplish discoloration below my knee and on the front of my calf.

I looked down and was surprised by what I saw. I couldn't remember banging my leg and certainly not hard enough to do that much damage; I ran my fingers over the dark skin and pressed gently. It was tender to the touch.

"I don't know how this happened, but I'm fine, just bruised." I looked at the captain and smiled, wanting to set him at ease; I liked him instantly. He was a big gentle man, with salt and pepper hair and warm intelligent eyes—the kind of eyes that I would have described as *laughing* had the situation been different.

"Check, make sure you're not hurt anywhere else." He insisted.

"Really, I am fine." But I stood and checked my arms and legs, both front and back to satisfy him.

"Good. And your dog—how is the dog?"

"Much better now, thank you. The cook gave her food and water, but she won't go to the bathroom. I walked her on deck...but nothing. I've started her on antibiotics; I'm afraid she has a urinary tract infection."

"You have antibiotics—good. She will be fine when we get to shore. We should reach Provo by morning."

"Provo! We're going to Provo!" I said in alarm—that was the wrong direction.

"Yes, we left South Caicos bound for Provo just this morning. The tide in South Caicos slowed us down, and then the storm."

"Please, you have to take me to South Caicos—my friend is waiting for me. He will be so worried."

"We can radio your friend; Provo will be better for you: there's a boatyard...everything you need..." he urged.

"Please, I have to get to South Caicos."

The captain was quiet for a moment. He stared at me but seemed lost in thought; he was torn I was sure. Should he continue on as he was supposed to or turn around and delay the entire shipment by at least a day? He sighed—the deep heavy sigh of one who has decided to do something that may not necessarily end well but feels right.

"We will take you to South Caicos."

I couldn't believe it; they were turning around. "Thank you! Oh, thank you."

He nodded in acknowledgement. "You are very brave. I have seen men who would not have handled the situation as well as you did."

"Thanks," I said, feeling proud but embarrassed.

"Do you have a transponder on board?"

"A transponder? No," I replied.

"Promise me you will get one in the future. A reflector is simply not enough. We saw your signal, but it was weak, and you didn't show a trail on radar." At my questioning look he elaborated. "A vessel traveling at any significant rate of speed shows a trail. You had no trail."

"I was hove to," I said. "I might have been drifting at about a knot, but that's it."

"That would explain it. Without the trail, we disregarded the blip as static caused by the storm. Not many sailboats go the route you chose; most prefer crossing the bank."

"I know...kind of wish I'd gone that route."

"Well...Don't worry about anything else. I have already contacted our corporate office, and we will take care of everything for you."

The day of our arrival was a blur of reports, surveys, investigations, and discovering that my boat was not covered by my insurance company at the particular latitude and longitude where the collision occurred. I wasn't worried; the executives of Mystic Shipping assured me that they would take care of everything.

In the morning, a small powerboat arrived to take the captain, Gary, Kia, and I to shore. *Gypsy Spirit* was already tied off at the government dock. We were met by a port agent who took our statements and told me that the police would be coming by to investigate and not to touch anything inside the boat.

The captain wanted to stay till Ed arrived and make sure I was okay, but he had to leave; they were already behind schedule.

The port agent urged me to go with a young couple from the sailboat *Nalani* for lunch, and although I was hesitant to leave the boat, I was glad I went; they were really nice, and it was good to have someone to talk too. Shortly after we returned, the insurance adjuster from Mystic Shipping arrived. The couple from *Nalani* stayed with me to be my witnesses and take pictures. The adjuster was by far the most unpleasant man I had met for as long as I could remember. He was rude and accused me of lying; he tried to say the impact came from the opposite direction even though it was quite obvious from the crushed metal which way the cargo ship had been traveling.

"You know we can get satellite images that will tell us exactly what happened," he threatened.

"Great—then you don't need to bother me anymore, do you?" I retorted as I reached the breaking point. "I'm done answering your questions. Go get your satellite images."

One Step Forward...

January 2007

Oasis Boatyard
Saint Augustine, Florida

Ed arrived minus his lady friend; he settled into the V-berth, and I, the aft cabin. Given the circumstances, our interactions became strained almost immediately. By *circumstances*, I mean that Ben was still very much a part of my life. When I'd tried to sever our ties, he accused me of having used him to bait Ed. I should have left it at that, let him say and believe what he wanted, but I couldn't and so it continued. He came to the boatyard daily, under the guise of wanting to help, but more often than not he arrived drunk. So he would hang around for a while, get frustrated and frustrate everyone else in turn. Eventually he learned to arrive just as we were finishing up and then accompany us to happy hour. Of course, he never had any money, and Ed watched in growing frustration as I spent much of my dwindling boat resources on Ben in an attempt to assuage my guilt. Ed urged me to put an end to everyone's misery by cutting Ben loose, and I tried on more than one occasion. But then Ben would call—out of his mind on drugs—and I would go to him, afraid that if I didn't, he'd get himself killed. Needless to say I wasn't doing so well emotionally, and my motivation suffered. I felt trapped and exhausted most of the time, like I just wanted to crawl into a hole somewhere and sleep for a very long time.

Amidst the drama I'd unwittingly created, we finished fairing and began priming the hull—it was beautiful, but almost a month had passed, and we still had one more coat of primer to apply before we could begin painting. The weather was really slowing us down: too cold and too wet for the primer to cure properly. I found a mast at a salvage yard in Saint Petersburg and began stripping it down for restoration. By the time Ed left in early March, we'd managed to get one coat of paint on the hull, and it looked quite promising.

Tugboat Sussex and barge towing Gypsy Spirit

A Tug, A Barge, A Rescue

April 2006 South Caicos, Turks and Caicos

Evening rolled in and still no sign of Ed. I'd been awake for sixty hours and counting. I sat in the cockpit, keeping vigil over the bay, till finally exhaustion overcame my resolve, and I slipped down wearily onto the cushion and closed my eyes. I was deep in sleep when Ed's boat glided silently into the anchorage. My dreams, like the sea on this windless night, were undisturbed as he set his anchor and searched the darkness for my boat. I couldn't see his frown or the haggard look about his eyes. Not till morning did I find Ed's boat anchored less than a quarter mile away.

"Kia, Kia, c'mon…wake up…look, it's Ed." At the mention of Ed's name, Kia's tail wagged furiously, and she pranced along the deck.

"C'mon, pup, let's go." We jumped from the boat to the seawall and walked its length till we reached the bit that led to the beach. Kia was in the water in a flash. I watched her frolic, but my attention was on Ed's boat. I could make out his familiar silhouette and saw him looking toward my boat; then he hoisted his dinghy over the rail and into the water. He drew the dinghy around to the stern and then lowered the outboard motor onto the transom. I called Kia, and we returned to the boat.

Below deck, heart racing, I knew my next action could redefine our relationship. I could play the helpless damsel and let Ed rescue me—I wouldn't be acting. I really was in distress, but helpless? I could let him know I needed him; I could break down into tears and let him console me…

The sound of the outboard motor grew louder as I filled the stovetop percolator. I felt a gentle nudge as the dinghy came to an abrupt stop at the jagged crack snaking down my hull into the water and heard Ed's ragged exclamation.

"Oh my god—fucking hell…" he mumbled. I poked my head out. He was stroking the hull; as he turned to look at me, I knew I couldn't do it. He looked vulnerable, and that scared me; I needed my cool, detached Ed. I would have to be the strong one now. I raised my head and smiled, wondering if I would ever regret this moment.

"Good morning, Pokey. You're just in time for coffee," I said in the cheekiest, most offhanded manner I could affect.

I noted the instant spark in his eyes and the arch of his brow as his face relaxed and his features flooded with relief. With that simple greeting, we'd stepped down from a major emotional precipice.

"Coffee sounds great, but only if you're having. Don't make it on my account."

"So what time did you get here?" I asked, feeling a bit like a character out of *The Twilight Zone*.

"Just before midnight."

"I tried to stay up and keep watch, but guess I fell asleep. I didn't want you to pull in and not see us."

"I didn't see you, and I thought maybe you'd gone to Provo. But then this morning… *I saw*…with the mast gone and the Bimini crushed, I thought…anyway, *Diesel Duck* and *Nalani* both hailed me and told me you were okay; they told me what happened. Then I saw you on the sea wall, but I couldn't see Kia…and I—"

"Hold that thought—I hear the coffee. I'll be right back."

This was going to take more self-control than I had. Why couldn't he be his normal, arrogant, unemotional self? It occurred to me then that I was nuts; I should have been having a breakdown, not analyzing my emotions and calculating my words like some bizarre chess game. I poured the coffee: two spoons Coffee-mate and three heaping teaspoons sugar for Ed; two teaspoons Coffee-mate, one teaspoon sugar for me. The clinking sound of the spoon against the mug was soothing.

Ed followed me a moment later down into the cabin. He looked around, then his gaze was drawn toward the bookshelves that we'd made on the starboard side just forward of the mast. He approached, then reached up and drew a book from the shelf: the Bible. It was standing upright and dry amidst the chaos and wreckage.

"How?" he asked simply.

I shrugged; I had no answer as to why this book stood untouched less than a foot from the point of impact when everything around it was in disarray.

"Huh. Strange," he said, and then placed the book back onto the shelf before climbing out into the sunlight.

I handed up the coffee, and joined Ed in the cockpit. We sipped quietly for a moment, then I lit a cigarette and began.

"You know what sucks—what really sucks?" I asked and inhaled deeply.

He looked at me waiting. I exhaled. The smoke lingered in the still air.

"It was all coming together...just like you said it would. I was sailing my boat, Ed...even in that storm. When I first saw those clouds, I thought, oh shit...but then—wow!—it was really something, you know."

He nodded.

I told him my story. He listened quietly to every detail: about the computer breaking and losing the charts, about my fright when the storm first hit, how I learned to balance the sails and hold a course, and my first quasi–heave to. He listened as I related the terrifying last seconds when I'd wondered what it would feel like to be crushed inside the hull. He was still listening an hour later. I paused for a second.

"Ed...*Gypsy Spirit* saved my life...She saved my life."

And then the tears began, and we were holding each other—no games, no bravado. I closed my eyes, feeling raw and exposed.

He held me. "It's over now. It's over. It's over now…" he kept repeating.

But, I didn't want it to be over—not like this.

I stayed with Ed on *Nini*. I had been staying with him since he arrived, and it felt right. I felt safe. He slept with an arm curled around me as though he were afraid I'd somehow disappear in the night.

We woke early and decided to spend the day exploring the small island a short distance from the shore. After a quick bite and cup of coffee, we motored out in the dinghy. The shallows were teaming with life. Not a single human footprint marred our pristine Easter Sunday beach. Tiny sea creatures blew bubbles and poked their heads out from the sand, then disappeared. Kia chased large blue crabs along the beach into the water, while Ed dove for conch and lobster, and I supervised. The water, a perfect shade of aquamarine, sparkled like crystal in the sunlight. We were alone, and for a few hours that day, I pretended that the accident never happened, that we were still on our adventure, and that I still had time to find the words and the courage to tell Ed how I felt. But then it was time to return to the boat.

We dined in silence, broken only by the sound of ripples lapping softly against the hull and the occasional cry of a seabird, on a feast of conch and lobster and macaroni salad, in the waning light and gentle breeze of early evening. We had almost finished eating when Ed put down his fork and cleared his throat as if to speak, then paused and looked away.

"What's the matter?" I asked.

"I think I'm going to leave on Wednesday." He paused. "Will you be okay here by yourself?"

I froze, fork halfway to my mouth. I couldn't believe it. But then I caught myself, put the fork down, and smiled.

"Yeah, of course I will. There's no reason for you to be stuck here—you should go on. I'm sure Mystic Shipping will take us back to West Palm on their next trip, so I'll be out of here in—what—a week or ten days or so. Definitely, you should go. I want you to go. Really, I do." Why couldn't I stop babbling and why was I so shocked by his announcement. I was the one who'd suggested he leave. I'd begun the day he arrived. I remember how it started.

"Ed, you don't have to stay here with me, you know," I'd said moments after I'd been able to stifle the sobs that had followed my story.

"Yes, I do. I have to stay till we know what's happening," he answered at first. That wasn't what I wanted to hear. I wanted to hear that he wanted to stay with me.

"Ed, we know what's going to happen. Mystic Shipping is going to load my boat on the next ship and take us home. We'll be fine. Why wait here with me till the ship arrives? You should go on," I'd said. But in my head I'd hoped that his response would be something like, "Are you on drugs, woman? I'm not leaving here without you."

What he said was, "Ya, maybe, we'll see."

My heart had skipped a beat then, but that had been the last of it, till his announcement of a moment ago.

I smiled brightly as my heart imploded. I ignored the dark wave of nausea that threatened to have me returning the bounty to the sea and said cheerily, "Well, this was a really delicious dinner, but I think I'm full; how about you?"

How does the expression go? "If you love something, set it free"? I had dared to believe—no, to hope for the fairy tale—but... My mind spun till I was dizzy and still had no answers. It spun till I was numb, and then it didn't matter anymore. We finished our dinner and chatted about the Dominican Republic and the crossing and what Mystic Shipping Company might do. We sat quietly together, looking up at the stars, alone in our thoughts, awkward in each other's company. Ed was already gone, and I understood his need for distance—especially now. I sighed, and with nothing left to say, I wished him a goodnight and climbed below.

My mind wandered restlessly, as I lay in darkness seeking sleep. He would leave in a few days. I would stay behind. I would stay with my boat till Mystic Shipping and I came to an agreement. I had known our travels would come to an end, but until now I'd managed not to look that far ahead. His presence had filled so much of my life. I wished it was all starting over. It had been a crazy, beautiful, frustrating, exciting, terrifying, blissful adventure—and I *had lived*. I felt more fully alive than I'd thought possible. It's odd that the very thing that made me feel so alive brought me the closest to death. Maybe to be truly free, you have to be willing to risk everything...maybe if I could love as fearlessly as I'd learned to live, I wouldn't have been crying silent tears of loneliness in the dark.

Ed left one week and one day after my accident. I'm not sure what time; I didn't want to know; I just looked out, and he was gone.

I was beginning to get a bit frustrated with Mystic Shipping Company. We had been going back and forth, quoting maritime law to each other, and trying to determine who was responsible for what. I guessed it was how the process worked. Maybe it would have been different if I'd been covered by insurance. They also told me they wouldn't be able to get the boat the next time they were in port, and they wouldn't be able to offer Kia and I passage. Their insurance prohibited passengers and livestock aboard in all cases but emergencies. I wrote again, asking them to stop thinking like businessmen and to please try and understand my position. If they wouldn't accept my terms, I would fight. It would not end like this.

I couldn't leave my dream behind and step back into my old life like a chastised child. My father urged me daily to leave the boat and find a flight home, but the boat would be ransacked within twenty-four hours and then there would be nothing left. Leaving there without *Gypsy Spirit* was just not an option.

I spent my days swimming and carving coconuts, transforming them into baskets and lanterns. On one I carved two sailboats and the sun shining above. I would give that one to Ed...someday. It was the way I'd like to remember our trip, the way I'd like him to remember. Seven more coconuts in varying stages of completion hung from the crushed remains of my Bimini in the cockpit. They would be gifts for everyone when I returned home.

Other than the occasional curious passerby and packs of street dogs, the area around the government dock was pretty much deserted. From time to time, in the evening, men wandered over from a nearby bar, curious about a woman alone on a boat. They wanted to know what happened and if they could have my lines and other equipment that I may no longer need.

Kia was my protector. She guarded our little home with fervor, yet somehow knew who to intimidate and who to leave alone. If I was afraid or got that sinking feeling in my stomach, her low warning growls ensued, and her lips curled back, exposing healthy, long white canines. Her shoulders hunched; her head lowered; and she leaped forward in short spurts along the deck, growling. Her protectiveness surprised me, considering the state I'd found her in a lifetime ago.

It happened about six months before I bought the boat; I had just taken Tanya to the airport after Christmas break. Rather than going home, I turned off and headed toward the Saint Augustine Humane Society. I don't know why; I hadn't wanted a dog. I was looking for a sailboat, and a spontaneous get-up-and-go life.

"Are you looking for a dog?" A red-haired woman asked. "If you are, I know the perfect one." At my look of confusion, she added, "I'm sorry, my name's Katie. I volunteer here."

"I'm kind of just looking. I can't have a dog. I'm going to be traveling. I don't even know why I came here actually."

"Oh, that's too bad. There's this one dog; she's really sweet. If I could have a dog, I'd adopt her myself. Would you like to see her?"

"I don't know. I really am just looking. I'll be traveling on a boat, and I don't think...Is she big?"

"Medium...You know, dogs make wonderful sailing companions. I'll have her brought out; she could use some outdoor time. Poor thing, they keep her separate. She's been returned a couple of times."

"Why?" I remember asking.

"I don't know. She's really sweet, a bit shy and nervous. They'll be putting her down if she's not adopted soon."

I remember the wave of panic that came right before I said, "Sure I'd like to see her."

I remember Kia being carried out to me; she was too large not to be walking, and she was thin—very thin.

"Why isn't she walking?" I asked.

Katie had shrugged and murmured something about Kia being "kind of shy."

"Kind of shy—she's trembling," I said.

"Why don't you sit down, and we'll put Ginger on the ground next to you."

"Ginger?"

"I call her that. We don't know what her name is."

I can still see the wild frightened eyes as Ginger crouched low and crept across the grass over to me. She had climbed onto my lap and buried her nose under my arm.

I remember thinking, I can't have a dog. This dog is already grown and probably won't like boats. My history with dogs is not good, and Mom isn't around to take over once the responsibility gets to be too much. Having a dog is a huge responsibility; taking home a dog with psychological issues is insane. "They're going to put her down"—the sentence echoed, and as my mind had said no, I heard myself saying, "I'll take her."

And the next thing I remember is looking for and finding a name—*Kianda*, from Angolan mythology, "Goddess of the Atlantic Ocean, protector of fishermen and sailors."

In a little while, we'd have to go ashore. I needed to email my letter to Mystic Shipping. I was going to give them until Monday to accept my terms. I felt a bit trapped and, like any cornered animal, when trapped, I fight. If I had to find a way to move this boat myself, I would. There was no way I would lose my boat, and I would not leave it behind to be vandalized.

"Ready, Kia girl?" I asked.

"Woof"

"What shall we do after we send the letter?"

Kia was running back and forth along the government landing. There was a large fish in the water, and she was in heaven—tail high and happy. At the sound of my voice, she trotted over cheerfully, wagged her tail, and sat.

"Up-up, Kia," I said, motioning to the seat next to me. She wagged her tail again but remained where she was.

"WUFF…woof, woof," *translation – c'mon let's play.*

"Okay, okay…hold on, I'm coming." The water was as clear as glass and teaming with life. It was a short dinghy ride to several tiny islands where Kia could romp and play and splash about. Only, we didn't have a dinghy anymore, and Ed had my outboard. Okay, enough. We could always climb down to the water from the seawall.

"Kia, I need to start listening to you more."

She woofed again in agreement.

Email forgotten we splashed and swam for the next couple of hours. Kia had me laughing with her antics. I tossed conch shells into the water. She swam and dove to retrieve them. She pranced about like a deer in the shallows, chasing the multitude of brightly colored little fish that she never managed to catch. She stuck her head underwater, and watched the fish, then surfaced, eyes blinking. I'd love to make her a snorkel someday—I could imagine it already—a long otter-dog swimming around with a snorkel.

In the waning light of early evening, I sat by the water's edge, tossing stones and watching Kia. She never tired, existing only in this one wonderful moment

"Come on, Kia, it's time to go home." Her expression reminded me of a petulant child.

Aw, come on, just a little bit longer...please, it seemed to say.

"Okay, a few more minutes." She splashed around a bit more then made her way over. I fixed dinner while Kia lay in her favorite spot in the cockpit, head resting on the rail, watching the world go by, savoring the breeze till darkness fell.

I stared off into the darkness, mulling over the events of the last year. It was a pleasant night; the breeze kept the bugs at bay. Judging from the clouds, there would be rain soon. Suddenly, a light from offshore pierced the darkness, dancing about like a firefly. I watched in fascination until it became appallingly clear that I was staring at the spotlight of a large vessel headed in my direction. It didn't make sense; the next ship wasn't due till Sunday.

"They don't see me!" I swung below, grabbed the spotlight, and began waving it over my boat and at the ship. I was able to make out that it was a barge being backed in by a tugboat.

"Kia, off," I demanded, pointing at the landing. She hesitated, confused and alarmed by the suddenness of my command.

"Now!" She leaped off the boat onto the landing. If I couldn't get the tug's attention, my boat could be crushed between the barge and the concrete wall of the landing. I had to be ready to jump ashore myself. I continued waving the light and issuing warnings over the VHF, not sure what channel they were monitoring. I could hear voices; they were shouting in Spanish. I couldn't make out what was being said, but I got the gist. Someone had seen my light and was warning the captain. Then there were several voices yelling and lots of commotion. A blinding spotlight clearly illuminated my boat. Slowly the progress of the barge slowed; then stopped. I breathed a sigh of relief as I watched them motor out into the basin. They turned, repositioning. The tug maneuvered the barge further down on the landing. Disaster averted, I joined Kia on shore. We made our way toward the barge; two men were securing the dock lines. They noted our approach and nodded in greeting, but nothing more. Then I noticed the boat's registration: the Dominican Republic—very interesting.

I awoke to the phone ringing. That was the one luxury—and I mean *luxury*—that I had there, but I was afraid to find out what the bill would be. I'd heard nightmare tales of bills from two to three thousand dollars for one month of phone service to the United States. For now I couldn't worry—this was my lifeline, my connection to my family and friends.

"Hi, Amal. How are you?" I said to my stepmom.

"I'm fine; your father wanted me to call to see what's happening with the shipping company."

"Not much; they don't know how or when they'd be able to load my boat without a rack or crane. They also said they can't take me or Kia. So I don't know, but a tugboat pulled in last night from the Dominican Republic. I think I might ask them if they would tow us."

"What!"

"Yeah—wait a second—hold on…Listen, Amal, I'm going to have to call you back. I see someone over there. I'll call you in a bit."

"Hello…Hello…Excuse me," I called, running up to the retreating figure.

"*Hola*," the man said, turning toward me.

"*Como esta?*" I asked, using all of my limited Spanish.

"*Bien…ah, espanol…*" he continued in a steady stream of Spanish.

"No, no sorry. *Yo, no hablo espanol*," I said.

"Okay, I speaking little *Ingles*," he said.

"You speak some English—that's wonderful. My name is Christine."

"Frankie," he said with a warm smile.

"Are you from the Dominican Republic?" I asked.

"*Si*, I am Dominican—Puerto Plata."

"Puerto Plata—that's the city you're from?" I asked, recognizing the name from something Ed said. It was a town about twenty-five miles east of Luperon, where Ed was.

"*Si, Puerto Plata*."

"Your boat is going to Puerto Plata?" I asked.

"*Si*, we make delivery *mañana* to Little Ambergris then Puerto Plata," Frankie gestured to the barge loaded with sand.

Another man appeared: a young man, thin and serious. I smiled, encouraging him to approach, but he kept his distance. I looked at Frankie questioningly.

"Ah, dat Jean Louis. He no speak *ingles y*...He 'fraid of jour dog."

"Oh, no, tell him not to be afraid. My dog is very friendly—really."

They spoke back and forth in Spanish. Frankie must have convinced Jean Louis; he began approaching very slowly.

"Sit, Kia," I said, to put them more at ease. Kia complied, putting on her best manners.

As he approached, I extended a hand. "Hi, Jean Louis. I'm Christine. Are you from Puerto Plata, too?"

"No, he is Santo Domingo...capital...long way."

"Oh, I see. I was going to Luperon. Do you know Luperon?" I asked.

"*Si*, Luperon very close to Puerto Plata," Frankie said.

"Oh, really? That's where I was going, but a big ship hit me. Now my boat is broken. See—no mast, and my engine doesn't work. I am stuck here. My friend is waiting for me in Luperon. I want to ask you if there is any chance you can tow me with you?" It was a long shot. Why should they help me? I couldn't pay them.

"Jou was alone?" Frankie asked.

"No, I was with my dog," I answered, pointing at Kia.

Frankie and Jean Louis conversed back and forth again. Frankie pointed at my boat as he spoke. They looked at me and at the boat.

"Jean Louis like to see jour boat," Frankie said.

"Sure, come on." I took them aboard and watched as they inspected my boat. Jean Louis was impressed with the autopilot, and I was struck by his serious, soulful eyes. He was as shy as Frankie was exuberant. Jean Louis spoke to Frankie. I waited as Frankie mentally translated.

"Jean Louis say he like jour boat. He want sail too. He say very bad what happen to jou. We maybe can help, but is up to captain. You speak to Captain Etienne."

"Captain Etienne, I see. Thank you very much. When do you think I can talk to him?"

"*Si*, we get him now," Frankie said.

Jean Louis said something to Frankie. "Jean Louis ask what wrong with jour engine."

"Tell him, I think there's a leak in one of the copper fuel lines running to an injector."

Frankie spoke to Jean Louis then said, "Jean Louis say you bring—he fix."

I looked at Jean Louis. He gave me a shy quiet smile.

"Thank you—thank you very much. I'll go get it."

I was on cloud nine as I went below to remove the fuel line. I couldn't believe that this might work, that these guys might actually consider what I was asking of them.

I removed the fuel line, and returned to the landing. Frankie and Jean Louis and another man were headed my way.

"Christine, Captain Etienne," Frankie said, making the introduction.

"Hi, captain. Pleased to meet you." Captain Etienne extended a hand, and we shook.

"My crew tells me you have a problem," the captain said.

I was relieved that he spoke English, although with a heavy Caribbean French accent. I explained my situation once again. He listened and seemed sympathetic. I finished and waited for his response.

"We would like to help, but the decision is not ours. You must call the owner. I will give you his number." He handed me a business card. It read: Sean Pratt, SandMine Dredging, and there were several numbers. I thanked them all once again, gave Jean Louis the fuel line, and headed back to my boat to make the call. I was more nervous now, because my hopes had grown and this would be the moment of truth. I dialed and waited, heart pounding so loud it was hard to hear when finally my call was answered.

"Hello," a deep male voice said.

"Hello, Mr. Pratt?"

"Yes."

"Hi, my name is Christine. I am calling from South Caicos. I just met the captain and crew of your tugboat *Sussex*."

"Yes, how may I help you?"

I launched into my story once again, speaking to the faceless voice, trying to picture the man. I told him about the accident and my days in South Caicos. I told him that all I had was six hundred dollars and that I would split it among the four-man crew.

I was breathless by the time I finished and the silence seemed to stretch forever.

I imagined in a moment he would say, "I'm very sorry, but with liability issues and insurance restrictions, you must understand..."

"If the captain and crew say yes, then it's okay with me."

I couldn't believe my ears. Was this really happening?

"Excuse me?" I asked incredulously.

"Yes. If it's okay with the captain, then yes."

"Thank you so much—you don't know what this means to me."

I could already picture myself entering Luperon harbor—like a soldier back from war, a conquering hero. I couldn't wait to see the expression on Ed's face when I arrived and motored up beside *Nini*.

"One thing though," Sean Pratt's voice cut into my happy musings. "We can't be responsible for your boat. If it endangers the safety of our vessel, we will have to cut it loose. If your boat is lost or sinks, you cannot hold us responsible. We need something in writing to that effect," he said.

"I understand, and it's definitely not a problem. I'll write a letter and give it to the captain. Thanks again."

My joy knew no bounds. I'd taken control of my life. I would see Ed soon, and this time I wouldn't be such a coward. I called my dad and Amal to share the good news, but they were less excited.

"Who are these people? How do you know you won't be kidnapped—or worse?" my dad asked, and I understood his misgivings. So I tried to give him as much information as possible about the crew, the company, and the boat.

"Were you able to reach the owner?" Captain Etienne asked.

"Yes, and he said okay—if it's okay with you. So what do you think?" I asked, with a huge smile already anticipating his answer.

"I think we have much work to do. I'll tell Frankie and Jean Louis," he said.

"Oh! Thank you!" I wanted to throw my arms around the man but restrained myself—definitely didn't want to give anyone the wrong impression.

I was waiting on the landing when Captain Etienne, Jean Louis, and Frankie arrived with another older man. He was introduced as Nino the Engineer. All four men spent the day helping me get the boat ready. I dove under the boat and cut away a line that was wrapped around the propeller. Jean Louis reinstalled the fuel line and tightened several connectors, then bled and started the engine. He rigged lights for the overnight trip, secured the boom, and straightened some of the stanchions. He secured a large shackle on either side of the toe rail to which we'd attach the tow line. With the help of all four men, the top half of mast was removed from the water and placed on the barge. The jib and roller-furler were removed and dismantled. I spent the day in a state of gratitude, overwhelmed that these people would take their time and energy to help a stranger. We worked till darkness fell; I gave them the letter and then we said goodnight.

"C'mon, Kia, let's go." We climbed out onto the landing for a late night walk. Lights flickered within the tug. I wondered what the men were doing, perhaps having dinner or making preparations for tomorrow morning's departure. I sighed, looking up at the moon. It would be full in another day or so, and it reminded me of how much I loved night sails. When the horizon was illuminated by the glowing light, you couldn't see the stars so well, but the line between sea and sky was vividly clear. Tonight I could still see the stars. Orion with his ever present sword and belt was there; no matter how far I traveled or how unfamiliar the place, Orion was there.

We returned to the boat, and I hunkered down into the cockpit, afraid to sleep below for fear the barge would depart without me. It didn't take long to fall into a deep sleep; the excitement of the past twenty-four hours had left me exhausted.

It was still dark when I woke with a start and looked toward the tug and barge. All aboard *Sussex* were still sleeping, and I breathed a sigh of relief. The air was heavy. It would rain today, and most likely there would be wind. But for now, everything was peaceful.

"Come on, Kia girl. Let's go for another walk."

Kia looked at me suspiciously. It was too early for us to be up and about. She hesitated, looking me in the eye before hopping off the boat to join me on the landing. I could see her mind working, trying to figure out what crazy scheme I'd concocted. She was right. This was about as far-fetched a plan as I'd ever had.

"Come on, I promise. It's going to be okay." We walked the same walk we'd walked every day for two weeks, yet this morning it was different. I walked with open eyes, knowing I was saying goodbye to a place that had been home for a little while—albeit a beautiful, exotic yet unappreciated home.

"I think we should get back, girl. We don't want to miss the boat."

"*Hola*, Captain. Good morning."

"Ah, Christine, Good morning. Are you almost ready?"

"Yes."

"Then please go start your boat and prepare for departure."

"Yes, okay, right away."

"I will send Jean Louis to help you."

Gypsy Spirit jumped to life. She knew that she must do her part. Jean Louis untied the lines that had held us fast to this concrete pier. I was at the helm and would drive her up to the barge, where we would secure her in a hip tow until we cleared the anchorage. It felt good to be on the move, and my adrenaline pumped. The captain was at the helm of the tugboat; Nino and Frankie were waiting for us on the barge. I brought Gypsy Spirit alongside; Jean Louis passed them the dock lines, then called to me and held out a hand to help me board. We ran the football field–length of the barge, and with a small jump, we boarded tugboat *Sussex*.

I made my way to the landing by the bridge, where the captain had instructed me to secure Kia before we left. I found her there, looking quite unhappy with her new surroundings. The wind was howling.

"It's okay, pup. You're okay. I had to take care of our boat. I'm back now. Don't worry."

The rain started: a drop here, a drop there, and then a steady drizzle. I was cold, but I had to stand my ground. The captain said that Kia must remain outside, and I couldn't argue, but I could remain outside with her. Hopefully he would feel bad and let us both in. The captain turned and looked from the enclosure of the bridge, and I thought he seemed somewhat agitated. He would obviously prefer that I go inside. Another moment passed, and he glanced again. I smiled in return, and he shook his head. The rain fell steady, and the wind blew. My T-shirt clung like a cold wet second skin. I wondered if I looked as pathetic as Kia. Several more minutes passed. Captain Etienne left the helm and called from the doorway.

"Christine, why are you sitting in the rain?"

"I can't leave Kia alone. She gets nervous since our accident."

"You are cold; you should go inside," he said.

"Don't worry about us. We'll be fine."

He shook his head again and returned to the helm.

"It won't be long now, baby. Just you wait and see." Kia was encouraged and gave me a slight wag.

I glanced surreptitiously in the captain's direction. He had the uncomfortable look of someone who was trying to sleep while being plagued by a mosquito. The wind whipped wet hair across my face. Kia and I huddled together in the deluge. I longed for the warmth of the galley, the aroma of coffee brewing and food cooking. I imagined it would be much like the galley of the cargo ship. My stomach rumbled at the memory of the tasty food aboard ship. I was hungry; Kia was hungry. When had we last eaten? I couldn't remember. Yes, we were as miserable as we looked.

At last the captain threw open the door and spoke the words I'd been longing to hear.

"Take your dog inside with you, but tie it up. I don't want it biting anyone."

I didn't need another invitation, and I didn't give him time for second thoughts. I untied Kia's leash and led her toward the stairs. "Thanks, I will. And don't worry, she doesn't bite. She's very friendly," I called out, disappearing before he had a chance to change his mind.

Inside the galley a diner-style booth awaited us. The built-in bench along the wall would serve as my bunk for the next few days. Seated on the bench, I took in my surroundings. I tied Kia to the table, where she promptly fell asleep. To my right a heavy metal door led out to the narrow deck. Through the open door, I could see waves splashing over the rail then draining out the gunwales. The refrigerator sat directly across from me—full, I was sure, of all the goodies we'd be eating on the trip. I wondered who did the actual cooking; with only four crew members, they must not have a dedicated chef the way the *Mystic Gem* did. The stove was to the left of the bench; a teapot sat precariously upon a burner. A thin wire attached to the cabinet above kept it from toppling over. I was surprised that they didn't have a more secure method for handling hot liquids, as it danced upon the stove.

The portside door was also latched open. A strong breeze blew in one door and out the other, and there was no escape from the wind. I huddled further back into my nook, wondering at what point they might close at least one of the storm doors. The sink and a series of cabinets stood in a row directly across from the stove. The men had probably eaten breakfast before we left. I glanced at my watch, hoping it would soon be lunchtime. I craved a cup of coffee, but didn't feel I had the right to go rummaging around, and so I waited. Frankie walked in, said hello, and then opened the refrigerator. It was not as full as I expected. Actually it was basically empty. There were a few eggs, some condiments, a half slab of some sort of sausage or salami, some bread, and a suspicious jar of something that looked like pickled meat. Frankie pulled out the jar, reached in, and pulled out a rubbery flapping piece of flesh. He bit into it, chewing appreciatively, then smiled and held out the jar, offering it to me.

"Oh, no thank you. Thank you very much, but I think I'll wait a bit."

Frankie shrugged and continued munching.

"I'm going to wait till lunch," I added, wondering when and what it might be and when it would be served. I eyed the cabinets, curious what lay within, and waited till Frankie left. I rose and poked my head out both doors. Once I was sure no one was coming, I checked the cabinets. I began to the left of the sink: Nescafe, powdered milk, and various containers of corn meal, pancake mix, and items I didn't recognize. In the next cabinet, I found tea, more instant coffee, and dry goods.

I wished I had thought to bring some snacks—alas, no munchies—but I did bring my journal, and while everything was fresh in my mind, I wanted to record every detail of these last few absolutely insane days. I glanced up at the clock: it was almost noon, not long till we reached Ambergris Cay. But we had to wait until high tide to bring the barge in to shore. Hopefully we'd unload the sand as soon as we arrived, spend the evening there, and head out first thing in the morning; then one more day and we'd reach the Dominican Republic. So far everything was going according to plan. I couldn't ask for more. I checked on *Gypsy Spirit*, and she was doing fine.

If *Gypsy Spirit* made it to the Dominican Republic, it would be a miracle. She was now completely dismasted. This happened as the crew attempted to anchor her offshore before docking the barge. Basically, the captain drove the barge into *Gypsy Spirit* while Frankie and Jean Louis screamed for him to stop. That was how things worked on this ship. The captain spoke English, and the crew spoke Spanish. The captain would scream orders that no one understood, and then the crew argued till the captain came and demonstrated what he wanted. They'd disagree and argue a bit more. The only time the screaming stopped was when we were underway and the crew was in the galley complaining about the captain and the poor conditions on the ship. I'd had some misgivings after witnessing the docking scene in the Turks and Caicos. My misgiving mounted upon seeing how far out the captain was planning on anchoring my boat.

"How deep is the water?" I asked.

"Can't be too deep; I can see the bottom," he answered.

Okay, so there was obviously no depth sounder involved in that calculation. The water was so clear the bottom would be perfectly visible even in forty feet. Finally after multiple failed attempts on the part of the captain to sink my boat, we pulled into the canal at Ambergris Cay. As it was too late to unload the sand, we made preparations to spend the night. But before I did anything else, I needed to get Kia off the boat. She needed to go potty.

"One minute, Christina," the captain said, raising a hand to stop me.

"Yes."

"You may go ashore, but you cannot take the dog—this is a private island."

"I have to take her; she needs to go to the bathroom," I said.

"Let her go on the barge," he answered.

"She won't; believe me, I've tried," I answered, starting to panic.

The captain looked irritated, but to my relief, he said, "I must speak with the developer. Wait here."

The captain walked down the ramp onto the beach and approached the small group assembled on the shore. He began talking to a particular gentleman who I assumed must be one of the developers. What if the man said no—that I had to keep Kia on board—what then? I waited anxiously for the verdict, and to my relief, after a moment the man looked my way and smiled. Captain Etienne waved me over.

"C'mon, Kia," I beckoned. "Be a good girl—first impressions count."

The developer was a great guy, and after a brief introduction, during which, with genuine interest, he had me recount my story, he graciously told me to make the island my home. He said that I should feel free to come and go, and that Kia was welcome. He offered me the use of their satellite phone, so I could contact my dad and let him know that I was alright. He asked if I would like a tour of the island, and upon hearing that I would, he arranged to have his general maintenance guy, Skip, take me around the following day.

I thanked him and said goodbye; then Kia and I made our way along the beach toward a little cove, where the crystal water beckoned. It almost felt as though we were back on one of our deserted islands as we spent the rest of the day combing the beach. We returned to the tugboat shortly before sunset, hungry and exhausted. Exhaustion was winning out, and

I longed to curl up on the bench and close my eyes. We must have missed dinner anyway, for although there was no longer any food, an amazingly large swarm of flies seemed to have taken up residence in the galley. Frankie was once again chewing a rubbery flap of meat, and Jean Louis was busy washing dishes. I wished them both a sleepy goodnight, then folded my sweatshirt into a pillow and scrunched myself down into the corner of the bench.

Skip arrived early the next morning, in a golf cart, to take me on a tour. Kia was to ride between us on the seat. As we headed off, he explained that the eleven-hundred-acre private island was being developed into a luxury community with home sites on the Caribbean Sea. The buyers would be members, and ownership would entitle them to all the island had to offer. He told me that the developer had also developed several resorts in Hilton Head, South Carolina. He took us to the most beautiful beach on the island and left us to enjoy it for a while. As much as I enjoyed the tour, I was antsy to get back. I was afraid they would unload the sand and leave without us. So when Skip returned to get us, I declined the rest of the tour and asked him to take us back to the landing. My fears were unfounded because they were just finishing up as we arrived. I saw Captain Etienne, and after thanking Skip profusely, I rushed over.

"Hi, Captain. I guess we'll be leaving soon, huh?" I ventured.

"We will not leave today. We must wait for fuel."

"Oh, I see." My heart sunk.

Another night trying to sleep in the fly-infested galley… Poor Kia, they swarmed around her like a dust storm, and they were intent on exploring her ears, her eyes, her nose, and her back side. She became crazed, spinning in circles, lunging out, snapping this way and that. Little fly carcasses littered the galley floor. Kia didn't miss her target.

The high point of the day came when Skip returned and handed Jean Louis a bucket of fish. I smiled, imagining tender white flaky fillets; my mouth watered—I could taste them already.

I imagined wrong. The fish were long and skinny, and Jean Louis chopped them crosswise, like cucumber slices, then tossed them in oil to fry—bones, skin, heads, eyeballs, everything. Even prepared this way, there was a lot less than one would imagine. Jean Louis cooked while Kia continued, like a demon possessed, trying to rid the boat of flies.

I watched the scene unfold in a hunger induced hallucinogenic state. Frankie walked in. I looked at him closer now, seeing suddenly a thirty-something-year-old Dominican man with close-cropped hair, kind of chubby, kind of funny, and full of mischief. Frankie was unhappy on the boat. He felt unappreciated and overworked. I got these sentiments directly from him on his many trips to the galley for snacks. When he wasn't eating, sleeping, or complaining, he sang, as he was now—loudly, especially while Jean Louis cooked. I sat, no longer swatting flies, listening to "Oh, Donna…Oh, Donna," which somehow blended rhythmically to the sound of the frying fish.

Suddenly Frankie stopped singing. He looked me in the eye, smiled, and said, "Jou know, jour boat was dis close to sinking," gesturing a hair's length between his thumb and forefinger.

"Really," I replied, trying to sound lighthearted. "How did that happen?"

"Well, jou see, de captain throw out anchor from barge. Jour boat go bang, bang, bang on barge. If I no cut line, jour boat bye-bye." He looked to Jean Louis for confirmation. Jean Louis nodded vehemently.

"Well, thank you, Frankie—you saved the day."

Frankie flushed and nodded graciously, accepting my praise, then picked up a fish slice and popped it in his mouth. A moment later Nino, the engineer, appeared as if out of thin air, and Jean Louis handed him a dish with several fried fish slices. Mysterious Nino—he moved quietly about the boat and seemed to be everywhere and nowhere at the same time. He would poke his head into the galley every now and then and flash me a toothless grin. Well, not exactly toothless—he had a couple off to the side. Nino was slight of build and lived in a pair of boxer shorts. He looked as though he'd spent the last fifty years in an engine room; actually he looked as though he were part of the engine room. He didn't say much, but seemed to see all; when he did speak, it would be to offer a timely pearl of wisdom, which he passed on to me via Frankie. Now, as Nino spoke, Frankie nodded furiously in agreement and glanced my way.

"What is it Frankie? What did he say?" I asked, knowing it had to be important.

"Nino, he say jou no let captain drive barge to boat. He say jou bring boat to barge. Jean Louis he help jou. Okay?" Frankie finished with a smile.

"I agree completely, Frankie. Please tell Nino I will do that—and thank you," I said. The three men smiled, happy that the problem had been solved. "The trick will be to find someone to take us out to the boat."

The fuel truck arrived early the following morning, and at last we were making preparations to be underway. As if on cue, a small motor boat bearing the insignia of the Department of Wildlife and Fisheries pulled up onto the beach. Frankie nudged me, smiling.

"Jou go now—ask them."

"I can't just walk over and ask them to give me ride," I said indignantly.

"Jou asked us..." he said.

He had a point. After a moment's hesitation, I made my way over to the three men.

"Excuse me, hi..." I had their attention.

"I hate to bother you, but I was wondering if you could perhaps do me a really big favor. I need to get out to that boat. Can you see it there?" I asked pointing. The men squinted in the direction that I indicated, out across the choppy sea. "I know... it's just a tiny speck from here. That's because it's out about two miles. Anyway, I need to get out there so I can drive my boat up to this barge." Their eyes moved to the barge in confusion. "I am taking my boat to Luperon. My friend is there." Blank stares. I made things worse the more I tried to explain. "I understand if you can't do it, that's fine."

"Come, we'll go now." The tallest man replied succinctly and nodded at the others.

"Oh, okay, we'll go now. Jean Louis! Jean Louis!" I called out. "We go now—okay?"

"*Si*, Christina. Jean Louis—he is coming with jou. No worry—just now. I watch dog—jou no worry," Frankie said.

"Thank you, Frankie."

After months of traveling at no more than six knots, the ride out to my boat was more than a bit exciting. I tensed up, which caused me to bounce harder and higher with each wave. Soon I was holding on for dear life. Jean Louis smiled, and I felt quite silly as everyone else seemed at ease on the boat. We thanked the guys and boarded *Gypsy Spirit*.

The wind was blowing, and there was a good two-foot chop. Without the mast to counteract the waves, the boat rocked and bobbed like a Weeble. We removed the bottom half of the mast from where it lay across the cockpit; then took the boom off and secured both items on the side deck. I started the engine; Jean Louis pulled up the anchor. Despite the damage it felt really good to be on my boat and to feel her move under her own power once again.

I imagined how things would play out once we reached the Dominican Republic. I'd motor proudly into the harbor. Ed's boat would be anchored just over there; I'd approach—slowly. He'd be lying half-asleep in his hammock. I'd idle by and then call out.

"Hey, Pokey, how's it going?" I could see the look on his face. I smiled. Jean Louis looked at me and raised an eyebrow.

I laughed. "I am just so happy, Jean Louis—very happy." He laughed then, too, but shook his head. He probably thought the crazy American woman has finally lost it.

Jean Louis pointed and called to me, "Christina!" I looked to where he pointed. The tug and barge were on their way.

"Okay, Jean Louis, this is it. Here we go—again."

I put the boat in gear and drove toward the barge. Frankie and Nino were waiting.

"*Gypsy Spirit*, you can do it. This may hurt a bit more, but you can make it. I know you can." My hands tingled on the wheel as our energies connected. I angled in, gradually bringing the boat alongside the barge. Jean Louis threw a line up to Nino.

The captain screamed from the helm, "Quickly, quickly, hurry!"

"*Si*! *Si*! We are coming!" Frankie yelled back.

"Jean Louis, wait—I need to get something!" Remembering the lack of provisions, I ducked below deck and grabbed the only readily available item—a bag of Dove chocolates. At least there would be something to eat. Nino grabbed my hand to help me up; then he and Frankie began letting out the harness-line. Within minutes *Gypsy Spirit* was being towed safely behind the barge. We had done it. The four of us raced across the barge and jumped onto the tug, then Nino and Frankie began letting out the massive towing lines until the barge reached a safe following distance.

Kia wagged with obvious relief when she saw me enter.

"When are you going to realize that I will never leave you behind, huh?" I said and plopped down onto the bench beside her.

"We're in the home stretch, pup; twenty-four hours to Luperon." I pulled a well-worn copy of Bruce VanSant's *Gentleman's Guide to Passages South* from my backpack and began reviewing the waypoints and navigational aids to entering the harbor. I carefully entered each waypoint into my GPS, then double-checked to make sure I'd entered each digit correctly. If the seas were still up, it would be quite a challenge, navigating the winding entrance to the harbor. There would be no room for human error.

Suddenly there came a shuffling thumping sound from the portside deck; I glanced over and saw that Nino had run a very large hose from the engine room out to the deck and over the bulwarks. Water was pumping out at an alarming rate. I wondered, in a vaguely detached sort of way—was there a leak or was storm water being pumped overboard? How ironic it would be—to go down on this boat after surviving a wreck on my own. Ah, well, I supposed the barge would more than replace the non-existent life raft if need be.

Nino looked up like a naughty child caught in the midst of some harmless mischief. He smiled reassuringly at my obvious concern. Lack of sleep had finally caught up, and even though I should have been wary, I couldn't muster up the energy to do more than smile in return. Potential disasters aside, the need for sleep outweighed even my gnawing hunger. I yawned, put my book away, and snuggled down, folding myself onto the hard wooden bench as best I could. With each roll and pitch of the boat the muscles in my stomach contracted and relaxed. I braced a knee against the table to keep from falling off the bench and closed my eyes. I could hear Kia's claws scraping along the floor as she struggled to stay in place. Time passed. Not quite asleep, though not awake, I was vaguely aware of people coming and going; I could hear Frankie's voice, and he sounded frightened. Note to self: *crew scared*—not a good sign. Ah, well, not much to be done about that. I drifted in and out of consciousness as the boat rolled and tossed and cabinet doors swung and the teapot danced upon the stovetop.

Ghostly white—sometime later I opened my eyes and found that everything was glowing white: the floors, the table, the counters, even Kia. I rose unsteadily and groped my way across the lurching cabin toward the light switch. Was this a dream? In my bleary state, it was easy to imagine that I was on some kind of ghost ship, but then my foot thumped against a soft but solid object. I turned on the light and studied the half-empty flour sack crumpled on the floor. It had fallen from a cabinet, and the wind had blown it around, coating every surface.

The captain clambered in through the storm door. "What is all this!"

I raised the offending bag for him to see. He shook his head and muttered something unintelligible as he shuffled about the kitchen gathering the fixings for a sandwich. I watched longingly.

"Would you like some?" he asked, holding out a half-stick of salami.

My mouth watered as I reached to take the proffered offering. "Thank you." I cut a slice, tore it in half, fed Kia, and then bit into the remaining half. I was almost dizzy from the pleasure. It was delicious, and I longed for more. But I could not ask—they had so little.

"Captain, would it be possible for me to take a shower?"

He nodded in the affirmative, then excused himself. He returned a moment later with a sliver of soap.

"For you," he said magnanimously.

From that simple gesture, it became even more clear, the scarcity of all but the most basic necessities. I now understood the lack of fresh food and regular meals. They were barely surviving, yet they'd done so much to help me.

"Thank you." I smiled, humbly accepting the gift.

Alone in the head, I held the sliver of a bar to my nose and inhaled the crisp clean scent, then peeled off my tank top and bottoms, eager to step into the warm spray. I slipped into the stall and felt my body relax as tiny rivulets caressed and carried a week's worth of sweat and grime promptly down the drain. The little bar of soap lathered generously, and I luxuriated in the moment, my fingers splayed, gliding gently over my body. When I reached my hips though, I stopped—the contours were unfamiliar. My hands spanned such a large area, and the curves had been replaced by sharp angles. When had I last looked in a mirror? I had showered on *Mystic Gem* after the accident, and that had been it; granted, I swam every day. My fingers continued their exploration: I could now easily span a thigh with two hands, but the flesh was firm, and I didn't feel weak; on the contrary, I felt stronger than ever, and my stomach was flat and hard. I smiled and tipped my head back, savoring the warm, pulsing massage on my head and face; and then just like that—the water stopped running.

"What the heck?" I turned the handle all the way. "No... no, we can't be out of water." I stepped out and tried the faucet at the sink—nothing.

"Great." I grabbed my pants and used them to wipe off the soap and dry myself. I felt much better but was definitely glad that I hadn't yet shampooed my tangled, matted hair—what a mess that would have been. I emerged from the bathroom just as the captain returned to make coffee.

"Um, captain, I think we've run out of water."

"Impossible—we filled the tank the other day," he said.

"I don't know about that, but there's no water now."

The captain went into the bathroom and tried the faucet. He reached into the shower stall and turned the handle in both directions. With an air of determination, he rushed into the kitchen and tried the faucet at the sink. Then, without a word, he stormed out of the kitchen toward the engine room. I suddenly recollected—the large hose just hours earlier, pumping water overboard—no, that couldn't that have been fresh water. I heard the captain shouting in broken Spanish, and Nino's mumbled response, then more screaming and finally the captain returned.

"That idiot used all the fresh water to wash the engine! Can you believe it?"

Actually, I couldn't, but it was rather funny under the circumstance. We were close enough to our destination that it was more of an inconvenience then a threat to life, and we did carry bottled drinking water, but no more bathing, toilet flushing, or dish washing. The captain sighed and climbed the stairs to the bridge, still muttering as he went. I grabbed my bag of chocolates, the GPS, and my binoculars and followed him up the stairs.

Everyone turned, in surprise. "Hi," I said, holding out a handful of chocolates. Frankie's eyes lit, and he took a couple. Everyone else took one, and soon we were all quietly savoring the smooth dark chocolate. I took advantage of the silence to pass out the four checks I'd written for one hundred fifty dollars each. While I wished it could have been more, the men seemed truly happy. We talked a bit; I gave the captain my waypoints for Luperon, which he programed into his GPS.

"Christine, in order to get you to your boat, we must pull the barge in like we did at Ambergris. It will be dangerous for your boat, as I'm sure you remember, and the sea is very rough."

I nodded.

"I think we should wait till we get close; then try to radio someone, have them come out and take you to your boat," the captain suggested.

"That's a great idea. We can call my friend Ed on *Nini*. He can come out in his dinghy."

I felt much better and handed out a second round of chocolates. We sat in quiet camaraderie, staring out into the darkness, watching for lights—five people whose lives were bound to the sea and for this moment in time to each other. A ship's light appeared in the distance. I passed my binoculars to the captain. They didn't have a pair on board.

"Hold your course," he said to Frankie, who was at the helm. "I'm going to rest. Come get me if anything comes up." Captain Etienne disappeared into his berth.

Nino slipped away soon after. Jean Louis, Frankie, and I sat together staring out into the darkness, searching the inky blackness for bits of light. In the following hours, I discovered that Jean Louis wanted to learn to sail and that Frankie hated life aboard ship—he was frightened most of the time. His dream was to go to America. I learned that the captain was actually the first mate. The actual ship's captain was ill and couldn't make the trip, which explained some of the difficulties in communication I'd witnessed earlier. I had to give the captain credit; he was doing exceptionally well given the circumstances. I learned that the boat had just been purchased, and this was its sea trial. The hours and the miles passed, bringing me ever closer to my destination.

Frankie smiled shyly. "Do jou have more chocolates?"

"Sure," I said, happy to be able to share something—anything—with them.

"We try radio," Frankie said, popping a chocolate into his mouth.

"Really? Already? Do you think we'll get through?" I asked.

He shrugged and handed me the transmitter. My heart fluttered in anticipation. I imagined Ed's surprise upon hearing my voice.

"*Nini*...*Nini*...*Nini*...This is the tugboat *Sussex*—over," I called into the transmitter. The crackle of radio silence filled the room.

"Jour name," Frankie suggested.

"*Nini*...*Nini*...*Nini*, *Gypsy Spirit*—over." Again nothing.

Frankie took the transmitter and began broadcasting in Spanish, also to no avail.

"I'm going to check on Kia, and I think I'll rest for a while." I left the bag of chocolates on the counter and turned away.

Kia's tail thumped contentedly as I lay down beside her on the bench.

"We'll be there soon, girl." The rhythmic thumping increased, then stopped as she closed her eyes. I must have drifted off soon after.

"Christina, Christina...Come—we are close."

I blinked my eyes against the bright morning light.

"Christina, wake up."

"What is it Frankie? What's going on?" I asked.

"We are very close; the captain speak on radio with the navy in Luperon."

"The navy? Why is he calling the navy?"

"Come now. Call jour friend."

"Kia, you stay, girl. I'll be right back." As I climbed the stairs to the bridge, I heard the captain speaking with someone on the radio.

"Christine, I am speaking with the Dominican Navy. I have tried your friend; there is no answer. They say the vessel *Nini* is in the harbor, but your friend is not there. The navy is sending a boat for you."

"Wonderful. I should go get my stuff together. Captain…"

"Yes."

"Thank you."

He nodded, and I raced down to the galley.

"This is it, Kia. We're almost there. It won't be long now," I said, stroking her head. "I need you to be brave for a bit longer." I could already envision her terror at having to jump from one moving vessel to another and then another, but we had no choice.

I placed my backpack by the doorway. Looking skyward, I saw the telltale mountain range but couldn't make out the inlet. I was glad that the navy would be there to guide me in. I squinted and saw a small boat with five men bouncing wildly toward us in the three-foot surf. I realized then that it was probably too rough for Ed and the dinghy anyway. They pulled alongside, and their small boat was buffeted against the tugboat. A small roundish man in military garb spoke. He seemed agitated and motioned for us to board.

"Christine, quickly climb aboard," Frankie said.

"But Kia?" I said, pointing at her for the military man to see. He became angry and started shouting.

Jean Louis appeared. "I go," he said, then jumped down into the boat.

"What's going on, Frankie?" I asked.

"The commandante say it dangerous for jou. They will get jour boat. Jean Louis help with the lines. They come for jou after. Is good, Christine—no worry."

Feeling helpless, I watched as the little boat bobbled clumsily toward the barge. Jean Louis climbed aboard; he would reel in the harness-lines once *Gypsy Spirit* was free. The powerboat bounced on till it reached my boat. Two men scrambled aboard, released the bowlines, and set my boat adrift. Caught by the wind, *Gypsy Spirit* sailed further away. I waited, straining to see a sign that she was moving under her own power. Slowly almost painfully *Gypsy Spirit* began lumbering toward us. The military boat, with its three remaining occupants, including the comandante, returned to the barge to retrieve Jean Louis, then motored up beside the tug. The comandante barked orders as the boat hurtled against our hull in the rough seas. Jean Louis motioned for me to pass Kia to him and then deposited her safely beside the comandante. He held up a hand to help me down, adjusted the straps on the life jacket he'd given me earlier, then he hugged me and was gone. I gathered Kia to my side, and the next thing I knew, we were bounding toward the inlet. I turned to wave goodbye; Jean Louis' sad eyes stared back at me from the deck, where he stood with Frankie and Nino and Captain Etienne.

As we drew closer to the inlet, the seas grew turbulent, and I feared being catapulted into the churning mess, but the driver, who appeared possessed, seemed not to notice. I prayed silently that he would slow down and noticed that the comandante was also not amused. He sat woodenly clutching his seat almost as tightly as I clung to Kia. I glanced up surreptitiously and noted next to the comandante was a man who looked like the Hollywood version of a handsome Latin guerilla.

He caught my glance. "*Hola*, my name is Handy Andy."

"Hi, I'm Christine."

"Were you really sailing your boat alone?" To my relief he spoke perfect English.

"Well, no, I was with Kia," I said, pointing.

Handy Andy laughed. "You are a very strong woman."

"Thanks. I really appreciate you guys coming out here for me."

Handy Andy translated for the comandante, who nodded graciously, then said something in Spanish to the driver. I looked at Handy Andy for clarification.

"The comandante would like to inspect your vessel."

"No, problem," I said.

Immediately upon entering the cut, the water became still. We snaked our way around and finally entered the harbor. There were boats everywhere and a marina and yacht club. Handy Andy pointed these out as we passed.

"After the comandante inspects your boat, we will take you to the marina for lunch."

"Thank you very much. But I'd like to clean up the boat a bit first."

"You have plenty of time for that. You must eat. Please, be my guest," Andy insisted.

"I really appreciate the offer, but right now my priority is to get the boat cleaned up and to find my friend."

"I understand. Remember, if you need anything, I am here for you. That is what I do."

"Thanks, Andy."

I scanned the water, my eyes flitting from boat to boat, looking for the familiar red and green of Ed's boat. Then at last I saw her; *Nini* sat at the far end of the harbor, and we were headed directly toward her.

"There she is! Do you see?" I asked excitedly.

"Yes, Christine, that is *Nini*, but your friend is not here," Andy said.

"I am sure he will be back in a bit."

"I hope so, but they say your friend went to Puerta Plata. He will be gone a few days."

My heart sank—so much for the grand entrance. Oh well, I had enough to keep me busy. He would be back soon, and the surprise could wait till then. At my request the navy guys anchored my boat as close to *Nini* as possible, then we boarded and followed the comandante down the companionway into the main salon. Smoke filled the air, and it smelled of burnt rubber; it was a chaotic mess with broken glass everywhere. I could not believe the devastation. It looked worse inside now than it did after the accident. Apparently, getting walloped by the barge and then three days of bobbing and rolling along had taken its toll. The comandante looked at me oddly. Perhaps he was just trying to put all the pieces together. I knew it was a bit unusual to find a woman and dog cruising alone, and even more unusual to find one that had been hit by a container ship and was now in your port. The comandante spoke to Handy Andy; then faced me with an expectant expression on his face.

"The comandante said he is finished here. The agricultural officer will come later to inspect your vessel and your dog. He said you go now to clear customs and immigration. We will take you there, and I will bring you back afterwards."

"Okay," I said. As we climbed out to the deck, I saw a familiar face approaching by dinghy. It was Eric, from Leaf Cay, and Salty, the dog. Kia went crazy with happiness and began prancing about the deck, much to the irritation of the comandante, whom she almost toppled into the water.

"Wow! Christine, you okay? How did you get here? Ed told us what happened, but I thought they were shipping you back to the States."

"They were; then they weren't; and now I'm here. That's the short version, and yes, I'm okay. Can I fill you in later? I have to go to customs," I said.

"Yeah, sure. Is there anything I can do?" Eric asked.

"Actually, I have a huge favor to ask. Could you please take Kia for the day? She hasn't been to shore yet, and it's dangerous for her here—there's broken glass everywhere."

"No problem. I'll bring her back tonight. By the way, does Ed know you're here?"

"No, I was hoping to surprise him. Guess the surprise is on me." I gestured toward Ed's unoccupied boat, with the dinghy floating behind.

"He left for Puerta Plata yesterday. I think he said he'd be back tomorrow. Anyway, I'll take Kia. You just focus on what you need to do. Come on, Kia. Let's go."

Kia didn't need coaxing. She couldn't wait to go with her best friend, Salty.

"Be a good girl, Kia. Thanks again, Eric."

"No problem."

The comandante, Papo (the driver), the two navy guys, Handy Andy, and I all piled back into the powerboat and headed over to the government dock. I was more relaxed now and began to take in my surroundings. This harbor was nestled safely between two mountains; no wonder it made such an excellent hurricane hole. The water was dark and murky; the anchorage was surrounded by mangroves. Several larger boats, including a navy ship, were berthed along the government dock. There were a number of smaller fishing boats and of course the assortment of cruising dinghies. We docked, then made our way down the dirt road to the comandante's office.

Gypsy Spirit... Phoenix Rising

April 2007

Oasis Boatyard
Saint Augustine, Florida

I smiled at the reflection shining back at me from my gleaming hull. Months of tedious work, five coats of Awl Grip, and no trace of the accident could be found on my beautiful, muted, cream-yellow hull. The waterline was prepped and primed, ready for the hunter green boot-stripe. The topsides were sanded and ready for primer. The teak would soon be varnished. Tanya and her new boyfriend, Abe, visited during their school break and helped me out quite a bit with the mast restoration.

The one year anniversary of the collision came and went, and Ed returned in mid-April. During his ten day stay, he built me a beautiful teak bowsprit and helped get the mast ready. I had extracted a promise from Ben that he would stay away from the boatyard—let us work. Consequently Ed and I got along really well and began making plans to meet up in the Bahamas. He offered to come back and sail over with me if I was nervous about making the crossing alone.

After Ed left for the Dominican Republic, I worked by floodlight late into the night, day after day. The teak was varnished; the interior cabinets, painted; the water tank, prepped; the chain plates, installed; and the stanchions, mounted. John welded and installed the toe rails. My only mistake—or should I say—my greatest mistake during the last busy days before the launch was that I let Ben back into my life. I was at a high point, and he seemed so low; I had to do something.

The mast was stepped and then on Friday, April 27, 2007, after seven long months in the boat yard, *Gypsy Spirit* splashed gracefully into the water.

She was my phoenix—maybe now it was my turn. As I looked upon my beautiful boat tethered proudly in her slip, I couldn't help but remember the day I returned from the comandante's office and beheld *Gypsy Spirit*, listing and broken, every inch of the hull scratched and dented.

Making friends in Luperon

Carte Blanche

April 2006 Luperon, Dominican Republic

I spent the rest of the day trying to sort out the mess on the boat. There was shattered glass everywhere: on the floor, the settees, the shelves; there was even glass inside some of the cabinets. I managed to get the boat under control just as Eric returned with Kia at nightfall.

"She's already been to shore a couple times, so she should be all set for the night."

"Thanks, Eric. Come on, Kia, up-up," I called her aboard. "I was wondering if you could possibly give me a ride over to *Nini*. I want to get the dinghy."

"Sure," he said. I climbed into Eric's dinghy, and we idled over.

"Thanks," I said, boarding *Nini*.

"Should I wait—make sure you get it started?" he asked.

"No, thanks. I'm going to stay here a bit."

"All right, goodnight. See you tomorrow."

I waited until the hum of Eric's outboard faded, then settled into the cockpit, closed my eyes, and breathed deeply *Nini*'s familiar safe scent. I was transported: It was June in Saint Augustine, and we were just getting ready to embark on our adventure. In a few moments, Ed would take me back to my boat; I would climb aboard, and we would set off, but for the moment we were together and I was safe.

I opened my eyes to the inky blackness of Luperon harbor then slid down into the dinghy and tried to start the engine—no luck. Ed had removed the emergency stop clip, and without it the engine wouldn't start. I looked around the cockpit for something to replace the pin, found some string, and was winding it around the shaft when through the night air, I heard someone speak.

"Can I help you?" a disembodied, distinctly British voice asked.

I had been so caught up in what I was doing, and it was so very dark that I hadn't noticed the man's approach.

"Yes, actually you can." I responded, "I am trying to steal this dinghy, but the owner has inconveniently removed the emergency stop clip. You wouldn't happen to have one lying around, would you?" I finished, frustrated with Ed for having made this so difficult and with the voice for questioning me.

"Ah, you must be Christine" was the amused reply. Before I could voice my surprise, he continued. "Ed told us a great deal about you. You are one very lucky young woman. My name is Derrick; I live on that boat—just there—with Esther. I am sure you will meet her very soon. I am keeping an eye on *Nini* for the old boy, and I think I have just the thing you're looking for. Hold on a second." He rummaged about in the dinghy and found a clip.

"Thanks. You don't happen to know when Ed will be back, do you?"

"I dare say it should be tomorrow at the latest. With you here I wouldn't be surprised if he rushed back tonight. He does know you're here, doesn't he?"

"Actually no, it was going to be a surprise," I said.

"Well, that could prove to be quite entertaining. Surprises all around."

I was a bit confused but agreed anyway. "I imagine you are right. Thanks for your help, Derrick. It was really nice meeting you. Goodnight."

Even Kia was restless; I don't think either of us slept more than an hour. The moist air weighed heavy and was ideal for the plethora of biting insects that we battled until the sun rose and drove them away. But by then, the temperature inside the boat had become intolerable, and even on deck, where the trade winds blew—there was no escape from the searing rays. Somehow, I would have to repair the Bimini and create some shade—fast. The metal arches of both the dodger and Bimini were crushed, and the fabric was torn. But the Bimini could be sewn, and with the corners tied to the handrails, there would be a moderate amount of shelter from both the sun and rain.

The trade winds blew steady as I worked into the afternoon, and then I heard the distant hum of an outboard motor. I looked up from my sewing and saw two people approaching in a small boat. One of them was Ed, of that I was sure. I continued sewing, trying to appear as nonchalant as possible, but my heart was racing with the thrill of the surprise in store for Ed. I heard his voice as he thanked the driver, and I looked up just as he was about to climb aboard my boat. I had played out this scenario time and again, imagining every possible reaction: overjoyed, incredulous, dumb-struck, even mildly surprised. I'd imagined every reaction except the one I got. He looked shocked, which, I guess, was to be expected. At first he said nothing at all, and I was on some kind of high, talking a mile a minute, telling him how I'd managed to get there. He listened and nodded. Finally, I ran out of breath and looked at him expectantly. I don't know exactly what I was waiting for—but something more than what I got.

"You're lucky the boat didn't sink—not the best idea. Anyway, you're here now," he said.

Like a raft with a pinhole—I was slowly but surely deflating.

"Mystic Shipping contacted me after you left; they said they couldn't bring the boat back to the States. They said they couldn't take me or Kia; they were going to give me airfare. I was going to have to leave the boat. I would have lost everything—the boat would have been stripped bare," I explained.

"If you would have waited till I called...I had a plan...I was going to suggest that I sail back; we strip your boat down; load all your stuff on *Nini*; and sail back to the Dominican Republic together. You could have relaxed for a while, done the tourist thing, and then flown home from here."

"I don't want to strip *Gypsy Spirit* down. She saved my life and if I can't bring her home, I'd rather give her to someone—like Jean Louis. I thought you'd be happy that I made it here," I said.

I stopped talking and waited; an awkward silence ensued, then he began.

"Of course I'm happy, but you have to understand...the situation changed."

"The situation changed?"

"When I got here, I went to Puerta Plata. Everywhere I went, I kept thinking 'I wish Chris could have seen this' or 'Chris would have loved that.' I even thought I should take some pictures and send them to you."

I listened quietly, but my mind was screaming. I wanted to shout, I'm here now, you idiot! We can see all the things you wanted me to see! Why don't you seem happy?

He continued, "Once I accepted the fact that you weren't here, I decided to focus on work. That's what I was doing in Puerta Plata; I went to see the guys I used to work for, find out if they had anything for me. I'm going to be doing some repair work on the same boat I used to captain. I'll be spending most of my time in Puerta Plata."

"I see," I replied.

"Listen, I'm really tired. I had a late night. I'm going to go relax for a while. We can meet up later and talk," he offered.

"Okay, cool, we'll talk later," I said.

Very calmly and with purpose, I finished sewing the zipper onto the Bimini. I attached the front corners to the handrails and completed my ragtag shelter, and then because I would not—could not—let myself get hurt, I got angry—very angry. It was one thing to tell me his plans had changed and that he wouldn't have any time for me. It was quite another to leave me stranded on my broken boat without a dinghy. By three o'clock I was fuming. I picked up the VHF transmitter.

"*Nini*...*Nini*...*Gypsy Spirit*—over," I called.

"*Gypsy Spirit*, this is *Nini*." His response was quick, as though he were sitting right by the radio. Obviously he wasn't sleeping.

"I would like you to come get me. I need to go in town, and I am taking the dinghy," I said abruptly.

"Okay."

In less than five minutes, he pulled up, looking rather sheepish. I climbed in across from him.

"Kia, be a good girl and take care of the boat," I called to Kia, and then looked at Ed. "I've made a decision. I'm going to spend a few days sorting out my boat; I'm going to explore the island; and then I'm leaving."

He said nothing. We drove to his boat in silence. I dropped him off; neither of us spoke.

I tied off at the government dock then proceeded down the debris-strewn road past the comandante's office, with the goat out front, past the ramshackle huts that served as stores, bars, and homes till I came to a restaurant. Seated just inside, I saw familiar face.

"Philippe?" I asked, walking up to the man.

"Christina? Oh my God, is that you?"

I nodded and smiled.

"*Mon dieu*, I hardly recognize you. What are you doing here?" he asked.

"Long story, Philippe."

"Join me for a drink and tell me the story."

"Sure, why not," I said and thought back to the day we'd met. I had just made an offer to purchase my boat. I was with Dave Huff, my boat broker and friend, at the Conch House in Saint Augustine. Dave introduced me to Philippe, a Frenchman, and his girlfriend, Nicki. They'd congratulated me, and we went to a Halloween party together. And that was the last I'd seen of either of them.

"Where's Nicki?" I asked, expecting to hear that she was on the boat or in town shopping.

"Ah...Nicki—we broke up a year ago. I am, as they say, *un* single-hander. I leave tonight. I just came to clear customs. How is it that we run into each other like this?"

"I know...it's really weird, isn't it?" I said.

"Not weird. It is a very nice surprise, *n'est pas*?"

"Some people might look at it that way," I said cryptically.

His brow furrowed a bit in confusion, then relaxed. "So tell me, how is it that you are here? Did you buy the boat? Are you with someone?"

"Hold on, hold on," I laughed. "One question at a time."

I proceeded to tell him my story, and Philippe was a wonderful audience. He was amazed with my tale of the collision, and unlike Ed he reacted with enthusiasm when I told him how I'd gotten the boat to the Dominican Republic.

"Who would imagine the quiet American girl I met in Saint Augustine on such an adventure. You must tell me more about this 'Head' character."

"Head? Who's Head?" I asked.

"Head—the guy you are sailing with," Philippe replied.

"Oh! You mean *Ed.*" I smiled.

"Yes, as I said, Head," Philippe repeated.

"Right. Well, not much to tell, actually," I said.

"Ah, *mais non*, there is much to tell—you love him, but you fear to admit it. He loves you…but he does not know."

"You're way off base." At his skeptical look, I added, "Really, I don't love him, and he certainly doesn't love me. Right now I'm not even sure if I like him very much. And, like I said, he was anything but excited to see me."

"But of course, this is understandable," Philippe said.

"It is?" I asked.

"*Mais oui*…He is ashamed. He feels responsible for what happened to you. Seeing you reminds him. He will get over it," he explained.

"There has to be more to it than that. I mean, he wasn't responsible for my accident."

"I know. You know. But he is a man, and that is how men are. *Mais*, tell me…I must know…Do you want him?"

"What!" I blurted.

"Do you want him?" he repeated.

"What kind of question is that? What do you mean—do I want him? That's the craziest thing I've ever heard."

"Do you?" he continued.

"No, I don't want him!"

"Good, then I will take you out for dinner. We will have a lovely evening and then we will make passionate love," Philippe said with a smile.

I burst out laughing. Philippe pretended to be insulted, then said, "See...you want him; you cannot imagine yourself with any man but him, not even an amazing lover like Philippe. Come, let me help you."

I did not admit to *wanting* Ed, but my curiosity was piqued.

"Just how do you intend to *help* me?" I asked.

"I cannot tell you; you must trust Philippe," he said.

"Trust you?" I asked.

"Yes, you will give me carte blanche, and I will give you Head," he explained.

"I don't think so. Tell me what you're going to do."

"No, I cannot. It will not work," he replied stubbornly.

"Philippe..."

"Have dinner with me," he suggested.

"I can't. I have Ed's dinghy, and he'd be worried if I didn't get back soon."

"We will return his dinghy, and I will meet this Head, and ask him to release you for the evening."

I laughed in spite of the headache that had been threatening for the last ten minutes. Against my better judgment, I agreed. By the time we reached Ed's boat, my head was pounding, and I knew that I was going to be ill. Ed emerged, looking slightly confused. I handed him the line and climbed into Philippe's dinghy.

I introduced Philippe. "Ed, this is my friend Philippe from Saint Augustine. Philippe, Ed."

"*Bon jour*, Head. I am very pleased to meet you. I have enjoyed hearing so much about you." He didn't give Ed a chance to speak. "You will forgive me, but tonight I will steal your dear girl. You have had her to yourself. It is so unfair, *n'est pas*. Tonight she is mine. This is acceptable, *non*?" Again he didn't wait for a response. "It was, *comment on dit*, a pleasure meeting you. *Au revoir*, Head."

I was speechless, and I would have enjoyed the completely baffled look on Ed's face so much more if I weren't feeling like my head was about to explode. Ed watched as we drove over to my boat.

"Thank you, Philippe. That was great."

"It was nothing. You did not give me carte blanche. I could have done more."

"What more would you have done?" I asked.

"That is my secret."

"Listen, Philippe, I'm not trying to blow you off or anything, but I really don't feel well. Could you please give me about an hour and a half to rest before we go out?" I asked.

Philippe looked at his watch, then said, "I will return at seven-thirty."

I laid down, hoping it would help, but my headache intensified, and I feared this would become one of my full-blown migraines—I'd been battling them for several years now. The moments ticked by in endless agony, and my stress increased as I saw that we were fast approaching seven-thirty. I prayed he would stand me up, but Kia alerted me to the fact that he had arrived. I popped my head out through the hatch above my bunk and called out.

"Philippe, I am not feeling so well." That was all I could manage before I had to run to the head. I thought he would leave then, but instead I found him standing next to me when I finally raised my head from the toilet.

"Philippe, please go. This is disgusting."

"No, nothing about you is disgusting," he said and helped me up from the floor.

He rubbed my back as the next wave of nausea racked my body, then he helped me to bed.

"Do you often get migraines?" he asked, concerned.

"A few times a month, and I have no idea what triggers them. They're not always this bad though."

"You rest; I'm here."

"I am really sorry about all this. You don't have to stay, you know," I said.

"I know."

But Philippe stayed. He held me when spasms sent me back to the bathroom. He rubbed my back soothingly as I tried to sleep. He forced me to drink liquid and crushed Tylenol, putting it under my tongue to be absorbed since I couldn't hold anything down. He took care of me. This relative stranger took care of me, while the man I wished were here, slept blissfully unaware of my plight. When it was clear that the worst was over and I could sleep, Philippe kissed my forehead and said he had to leave. He said he found me tempting even in this condition. I laughed, and he smiled, promising to come back later.

Philippe returned the next morning; we took Kia ashore and then toured the harbor. He introduced me to his friends. "So you won't be alone when I leave," he said, just before dropping

Kia and me off at *Nini*. We hugged, said goodbye, promised to meet up someday in the States, then Philippe sailed away.

Within a couple of days, things returned to "normal" between Ed and I; I'd gotten over my anger, and he didn't seem so distant. He urged me not to leave in a huff, suggested that I try to see some of the island before I returned to the United States. By then I'd realized that getting home with Kia and my belongings would not be as easy as I'd initially thought. There were flying restrictions for Kia, due to the heat, and most airlines wouldn't take dogs. I could not find one U.S. carrier with a climate-controlled cargo area. Also I would be limited to two suitcases. I decided to try and find a sailboat heading north, back to the States—one that would be willing to take Kia and all my gear. Around that time, Mystic Shipping Company and I came to an agreement. I signed the appropriate release, and they transferred the funds into my account via my attorney back in the States. As had happened before in West Palm, Luperon began to feel like home, aside from the fact that I was living on a mess of a boat that was tipped about ten degrees to keep the crack in the hull out of the water.

The hardest part of life in Luperon during the first few weeks was what I called the *tourist attraction factor*. Everyone wanted to see the mangled boat and the woman and dog that had survived. At any time of day, I'd surface to find a tender quietly circling my boat like a shark. As I've said before, I prefer to move about invisibly, and my latest exploits had most certainly made that impossible; there were fingers pointed and whispers. "That's her; that's the one." Maybe it would have been different if I'd achieved notoriety for some heroic act or talent. Stories abounded regarding the details of the accident, and when the details were unknown or hazy, they were creatively embellished, oftentimes with me sitting within earshot. One afternoon I was with Ed having lunch at the yacht club. A party of six was seated at the next table, and I couldn't help but overhear their conversation.

"I heard she was floating out there for days. She lost her mast in a storm and ran out of fuel."

"I thought the boat was hit by a barge or something. They salvaged the boat and called the navy."

"Wasn't it a container ship?"

"A container ship—my god—can you imagine?"

"How did it happen?"

"You know—sailing alone. She was probably asleep. Those single-handers think they can just set their boats to sea, go below, and take a nap."

"Most of them are a little off; I mean, can you imagine spending all that time by yourself?"

"So what's she doing now? Where is she?"

"I don't know; the boat is in pretty rough shape; the navy and tugboat company are both claiming salvage rights."

"She's damned lucky someone found her. She was out of food and water. Another day or so and…"

"She had a dog with her. Can you imagine? Endangering your own life is one thing, but a helpless animal."

"Is the dog okay?"

"I'm not sure, but I heard…"

And so it went, until in time, as with all things, the novelty wore off, and we simply slipped ever-so-quietly into the landscape. I was most happily invisible once again.

Ed and I began sightseeing. We made several trips via *motto concho* (scooter), *publico* (public car), and *guagua* (bus) to the bustling port town of Puerta Plata. Typical guaguas were midsized, four-door vehicles and often carried up to eight adults. After the first trip, I learned that half the adventure was in getting there. If I was to choose a single statement to describe the Dominican people, I would say they had joie de vivre that I'd never seen anywhere else; and nowhere was this more obvious than in the public transportation system. Music played in taxis and on the bus. More than once I saw someone dancing in the aisle during the evening commute. People laughed and talked, even to complete strangers. An old woman would reach out to jostle a baby or hold the infant while a young mom saw to the needs of her toddler. The people I met were warm and open. I made friends and started learning Spanish, and although I had a vague sense of being trapped, I really started enjoying my time in the Dominican Republic. The country was beautiful; the landscape, lush, green, and fertile. Coffee, tea, and some of the most beautiful roses in the world grow in the mountains of the Dominican Republic. There was much poverty, but all in all the people seemed exceptionally happy.

As far as going home was concerned, it became apparent rather quickly that I wouldn't have much luck finding a boat, most were heading south at this time of year. I spent a great deal of time at the Verizon store in Luperon, using their computers, trying to find a flight. Not that I wanted to leave immediately; I just wanted to know I would be able to. Most flights, all the ones from Puerta Plata anyway, left too late in the day, when the temperatures had risen and Kia would be denied boarding.

I even explored the option of flying to Europe, then to the U.S., because they had climate-controlled flights, but Kia did not meet the vaccination requirements. Several people suggested I leave her behind then have her sent over in the fall or winter, but I couldn't do that; she needed me, and truth be told, I now realized how much I needed her.

At last I found an American Airlines flight departing from the capital at six in the morning. The temperature at that time of day could vary anywhere from about seventy-three to eighty-five degrees; we would have to take a chance and hope that it would be cool enough on that day to get Kia on the flight. Eighty-five degrees was the cut off. The trip to Santo Domingo by car would take us ten or more hours, south across the mountains to the Caribbean Sea. We would make the journey, then find out if we'd be able to board. With no other option, I purchased the ticket and began jumping through hoops to get Kia approved to fly home. If all went well, I would be home for Father's Day.

My friend Marina offered to spend her vacation with me in the Dominican Republic. She was going to bring four empty suitcases, nested inside each other, then she'd return with two, and I would bring the other two. Her carry-on would suffice for her own belongings, and in that manner, I'd be able to return with almost all of my valuables. With my friend's impending visit, I began to regard my stay as a holiday. I couldn't expect her to stay on the boat—it was hard enough for me—so I rented a one-bedroom patio apartment with a swimming pool and a garden, and soon I was feeling like my old self.

Ed and I picked Marina up from the airport, and we spent several days relaxing and partying in the seaside resort towns of Sosua and Cabarete. But then we had to return to Luperon, because Ed had a boat delivery to make and would be departing for Cuba early the next morning.

"Can you believe the nerve of him? Acting hurt simply because I'm not meeting him at the dock at five-thirty in the morning to see him off," I said to Marina, once we were finally alone in my apartment.

"You should."

"Why?" I scrunched up my face.

"Let him know you care and maybe give him a nice, big kiss goodbye."

"You're funny."

"That's it! I love it. You're going to kiss him," she stated and, at my look of panic, continued, "You're going to meet him at the dock tomorrow morning; you're going to give him a hug goodbye; and then you are going to kiss him—on the lips. That simple. I mean really, I don't understand what the big deal is… Can you please try and act normal for a change."

"Marina, I can't…I…"

She held up a hand. "I don't want to hear it; I'm sick of this. Do you realize that you are going home soon? He's going back to South Africa. It's over—you have absolutely nothing to lose. Just do it."

It's over…It's over…It's over…It's over…Marina's voice reverberated, but it wasn't her voice—it was the incessant ringing of the alarm clock, alerting me to the fact that it was 5:15 a.m. I jumped out of bed, brushed my teeth, splashed water on my face, and darted out the door. He'd probably be gone already. I was out of breath by the time I reached the marina and slowed to a walk—wouldn't do to arrive panting. As I rounded the corner, I saw him; more importantly, I saw the way his eyes lit when he realized that I'd come.

"Well, good morning," he said brightly.

"Hi," I answered, thinking of *the kiss* and feeling suddenly shy. My face burned, and I found it hard to make eye contact. Thankfully Ed didn't seem to notice; he was preoccupied with the upcoming journey.

"I should be back in less than a week. The weather looks good; the delivery will be easy." He was flying to Cuba, relocating a charter boat from there to the Virgin Islands. I would have loved to have gone with him, but for Kia. "Take care of yourself and the hound."

"I will and you...stay safe...okay." Time was running out. I had to make my move, but he was looking at me strangely... Did he know what I was planning?

"All right, then—I guess this is goodbye." He started to turn away.

"No, wait." He stopped and tensed almost imperceptibly, but I noticed, and my throat constricted. "Give me a hug." I managed to squeak out the words.

He relaxed and turned to me with a smile. We embraced, and I held him tight; my heart pounded no less fiercely than it had in the face of the elephants on the horizon. "I'll really only be gone a week," he assured me, thinking that this was the reason for the death grip.

"I know," I said and pulled back. This was it—now or never. I looked into his eyes, then at his lips; I moved in closer, making my intention known, closer, and then I saw his panic. We were but a breath apart when I turned slightly and my lips met the sensitive corner of his mouth, and there I placed a tentative kiss, then stepped away quickly. We mumbled our goodbyes, and I stumbled home not quite sure if I'd succeeded or failed.

"What do you mean 'sort of'? Did you kiss him or didn't you?"

"He looked really freaked out, so I sort of kissed him quickly on the corner of his mouth."

"And?"

"And it was nice," I said with a smile. "And...I have an idea," I continued conspiratorially. "Ed lent me his camera," I said, holding up a small digital camera. "Mine broke in the accident. I think maybe we need to take some pictures."

"What kind of pictures?"

"Well, let's just say, I'm in the best shape of my life, and it would be a shame not to get some photos to look back on when I'm eighty or so...Sure hope I don't forget to take them off the camera before I give it back to him."

"You're really bad! And always pretending to be Little Miss Innocent."

I smiled with the thrill of my plan.

...Two Steps Back

June 2007 | Intercoastal Waterway, Florida
-To The Bahamas

Call me a glutton for punishment, an idiot bound on self-destruction, a coward afraid of love; call me all three, and it would be true; knowing all I knew, I still agreed to bring Ben on the maiden voyage of *Gypsy Spirit* to the Bahamas. Maybe I did it out of guilt for not caring about him as he did me, or the belief that the trip might be good for him, a once in a lifetime opportunity he'd never manage on his own—I can't say it was completely one or the other. Anyway, he promised to control his drinking, and he was supposed to save one thousand dollars to bring on the trip.

Ed was not thrilled with the prospect of spending time with Ben. "If he can act normal, it will be fine" was his only input on the matter. Ed would sail from the Dominican Republic, where he left his boat last year, to Green Turtle Cay. Tanya would fly to the Bahamas via Florida.

Ben and I bickered the entire way down the Intercoastal, as he drank what was left of his cruising fund. I felt like the parent of a troubled teen and was torn between the desire to dump him off at the next dock and my need to see things through. If I could only get him away from temptation long enough, perhaps everything would be okay.

Once we reached West Palm, I was able to arrange work for Ben. He lasted three days, then began to complain that I was stalling, trying to prevent him from getting to the Bahamas in time for the regatta. Actually, I was watching weather, trying to ensure as comfortable a crossing as possible, and the weather in my opinion had not been ideal. He attempted finding passage with another boat but was unable, and finally after many second thoughts on my part as to the sanity of this undertaking, we crossed the Gulf Stream on July 2, 2007.

This was supposed to be a joyous time, a triumphant return to cruising, but Ben was driving me insane, and I was getting migraines almost every day. He was drinking very heavily, and I realized that he had spent the last of what he earned before we even left the United States. Once we reached the Bahamas and met up with Ed and Tanya, things got worse. Ben took to spending his days alone on the boat, drinking and dancing on deck. He'd wait till Tanya and I left, and then raise his gargantuan Gators flag to mid-mast and scream, "Go Gator Nation!" to every passerby.

One afternoon, he decided to honor us with his latest "Ed impression." With his wrist held high and bent at a ninety-degree angle, he attempted to mimic an effeminate gay man.

"Hi, I'm Ed." He swung his hips and continued, "I am so cool, I just don't know what to do with myself."

During his drunken antics, he managed to: break a stanchion while trying to jump off the boat, impale himself with a fishing hook and remain impaled for the next three days, burn the cockpit table by lighting the Coleman camp stove upside down, and almost choke to death on his own vomit as he lay passed out in his berth. Of course I'd long since realized the extent of my error, but it was too late, and everyone had been impacted.

I was emotionally spent, but in all fairness, it was not only because of my dealings with Ben. I had major unresolved issues in regard to the collision, like an intense need to control all aspects of the journey. And with sailing, the one thing I had virtually no control over was the weather. Especially during the summer, with the intense heat and moisture, storm clouds formed suddenly and spawned violent thunderstorms. Winds could easily top sixty miles an hour, and waterspouts were not uncommon. Just before we left Saint Augustine, a tornado ripped through town; I was on the boat and saw the gray swirling mass seconds before it hit and literally threw my boat on its side against the dock in one jarring motion, then stripped the deck bare. My brain was stuck on high alert.

"I can't take this anymore; I have to go back," I said suddenly. We were sitting on Ed's boat, Tanya and I, enjoying a cold soda.

"Are you nuts Mom? You just got here."

"I don't mean today, honey. I'll stay till you leave. But this is crazy; I can't do it."

"Hey, hey…What am I? Chopped liver? I just sailed here all the way from the Dominican Republic to meet you…and you're going to leave?" Ed asked incredulously.

"I'm so sorry, but what else can I do?"

"Tell him to go home," Tanya said.

"How? He doesn't have any money."

"Buy him a ticket. You can't end the trip because of him," she continued.

"Remember when I told you to collect airfare and put it aside," Ed said. I nodded, and he continued, "This is why. Never take passengers without collecting airfare. If they behave, give it back; if they don't, buy them a ticket. Spend the money; send him home."

"I can't. When you leave with someone, you return with them. I was wrong to bring him, but I can do the right thing and take him back."

"Mom, there is no right thing anymore—it's all wrong. And you are not responsible for him—he's not a baby. Yeah, it was really dumb to bring him, and I don't get it. But it's not your job to take him home. Ed's right; buy him a ticket."

I glanced toward my boat; Ben was dancing wildly along the deck, swinging in circles around the shrouds.

"Ya, I don't get it either," Ed said, following my gaze, and looking at me with that old arrogant expression that I loved and hated so much. "What about your book? I thought you were going to work on the book."

"I can't work on anything right now. I am brain-dead."

Tanya left at the end of the week, and I prepped for the return to Florida. On departure day; I climbed down into the dinghy and motored slowly over to Ed's. I was dreading this goodbye.

"Please, don't be mad at me. I have to go, but I am not leaving you…I'm just leaving the Bahamas."

"I don't understand, but, hey, do what you have to do." He sounded cold, and my heart constricted a little bit more if that was possible.

"You are mad at me…Please, don't be," I said, as I bent forward to kiss him goodbye.

I didn't understand what I was doing either; I was running on instinct; I had to get back to the States. Part of the reason was Ben, but the rest was my anxiety over what could happen. The trip had been perfect from a mechanical standpoint—I couldn't ask for more. But the demons were there, in my head, taunting me, reminding me of what could happen, and telling me I'd only be safe when we reached home.

Ben and I sailed to West End, waited for weather and crossed. Several days later, we arrived in Saint Augustine. I hauled my boat, breathed a sigh of relief once she was sitting safely on jack stands, rented a truck, and left for Boston without looking back. I was free: of Ben, of the weather, of everything—but at what cost? If I'd almost lost Ed once before, I most certainly had done so now. Would I never learn? Was I destined to repeat this pattern of running away whenever my heart's desire was within reach? Hadn't I done virtually the same thing in the Dominican Republic just one year ago?

View of Luperon Harbor from the yacht club

The Long Goodbye

June 2006 Luperon, Dominican Republic

The photos, left on the camera, accidentally on purpose, had worked their magic. I'd thanked Ed and given him the camera on the morning of his return from the boat delivery. A few hours later, he stopped by my apartment. I was packing in preparation for my departure later that night. I opened the door and knew immediately, by the hesitantly hopeful twinkle in his eyes, that he had seen the photos.

"I think you may have forgotten to delete some of your pictures," he said, holding up the camera.

"Really? Let me see."

He pushed the power button and advanced slowly, one by one, through five photos.

"Wait. Go back. One more...there! That one's my favorite. What do you think?" I asked. It was a simple photo, inspired by a painting I'd seen somewhere. It was taken from the back; I was seated nude on my heels with my legs folded beneath me. My head was thrown back and my long hair fell almost to the heart-shaped curve of my bottom. My arms were extended above my head, and I was pouring water onto my hair and down my back from a large conch shell. I thought it quite artistic, and in the boldest moment of our entire time together, I said, "I didn't forget those photos Ed—I took them for you." My heart was racing, partly from excitement and a sense of danger, but mostly in reaction to the look I saw in his eyes.

"Very nice," he said matter-of-factly. "I like this one, too," he noted of a fairly provocative photo in which I was staring directly into the camera, seated on a chair, wearing a little black teddy and stiletto feathered pumps. "Far cry from the innocent school girl I've been traveling with."

"Maybe—just a bit."

"How did you do this? Who took these pictures?"

"Well it wasn't the comandante…Marina, of course. I asked her to take some sexy pictures."

"Hmm…interesting. I was wondering…Would you like to have dinner with me tonight on *Nini*? I can pick you up around seven, and I'll have you back by midnight, in time to catch your cab."

"I would like that very much."

I stowed my luggage at the marina, where the cab would pick me later that night. Ed arrived, and I stepped into the dinghy feeling suddenly shy; he was quiet as well; we were like two children on a first date. When we reached *Nini*, I held the dinghy in place for Kia to jump aboard, then climbed up and held the line for Ed. Kia found her favorite spot in the cockpit and curled into a ball, oblivious to the palpable energy. I proceeded down into the salon and watched while Ed put the final touches on the dinner he'd prepared. He poured us both a drink; we sipped and chatted about this and that though nothing in particular.

"This is weird…I can't believe we're here like this…now. I always thought you were afraid you'd turn to stone or something if you got too close to me," I said.

He gave me a wry smile. "I was just trying to do the right thing," he said almost sadly. "We've known all along that I was going back to South Africa, and you're leaving for Boston. Who knows if we'll ever see each other again? I didn't want to hurt you, and I most certainly didn't want you hanging onto my leg, begging me to stay, as I fought my way onto the plane." He finished with his normal arrogant flair, trying to lighten the mood.

"Well, I guess I've eliminated that concern, since I am the one leaving first. Be careful, or you'll be the one clinging."

I kept glancing at the clock every few minutes, afraid of what I'd see; time was moving too fast; in less than four hours, we would say goodbye. We once had all the time in the world, but now it had come down to these last two hundred forty minutes. I gulped down the remainder of my drink.

"Could I have another, please?"

After the second drink and a half-hearted attempt to eat dinner, I stole a fleeting glance at the man who had shaped a large part of my world for some time now, and decided that the time had come. His hand was resting on the settee; I moved mine closer so that our fingers touched…then waited. He turned his hand over, so that it rested palm side up—gently I placed my hand in his—fingers splayed and then intertwined… For a few brief hours, time stood still on the night of my departure.

"Oh my god, Ed, it's almost midnight. I have to go; I'm gonna miss the plane," I cried as I gathered my belongings and made some attempt to sort out my disheveled appearance.

"Relax, the cab will wait. I'll get you there in time…Don't worry."

We set off in the dinghy. I held the flashlight to light our way through the darkness toward the marina.

"Ed, I just want to say…thank you…thank you for everything. It's been great—really it has."

"Hold on. After what just happened, you're leaving me with 'hey, it's been great, thanks'?"

"What am I supposed to say? I was trying to make it easy for you."

"Easy for me…none of this is easy."

"I know. But you'll get back to South Africa, and before you know it, you'll meet someone, and everything will be great."

"I'm not going to meet someone; I don't want to meet anyone."

"All right, then why don't we just wait and see what happens," I said, and my heart soared.

The cab was waiting when we arrived, so there would be no long goodbyes. We were running late and had to hustle to get my bags and Kia's crate loaded into the van.

I turned to the driver. "Could I have a minute, please?"

He looked at his watch impatiently. "We have a long drive—be quick."

"Come here. Give me a hug," I said. How formal we were once again.

Ed wrapped me in a warm embrace. "Have a safe trip home. I'll call you; we'll talk; don't worry about anything."

I nodded. "Okay, goodbye. I am going to miss you." A final kiss, then he let me go, and I walked toward the cab. He closed the door after me and then we were moving. I looked back. Ed stood glued to the spot. I watched him watching me, until we turned the corner, and he was gone.

Gypsy Spirit Bahamas bound at sunrise

Redemption

April 2010

Saint Augustine, Florida
-To The Bahamas

Two and a half years passed since the fiasco with Ben in the Bahamas and although we kept each other up to date, and managed a visit or two, Ed and I rarely spoke. One year he spent Christmas with me in Boston, and then we drove down to Saint Augustine together.

As he was leaving, he said, "I think we might had made a go of it…you and I, if it had not been for Sophie; I'm only just over her now."

I didn't know what to say—so I said nothing at all and watched him drive away.

A couple of years later, he called to wish me a happy birthday, and with a half a world between us, I plucked up the courage to say, "Strange as this may seem, looking back I think that ours may have been the best relationship of my life."

For years we'd played the game—over and over. We danced the *comfort zone tango*— alone, in circles around each other: advance, retreat; advance, retreat; no winner, no loser; nothing lost; and nothing gained. And then one day, the music stopped, and all that remained was the silence between the notes.

Time passed, I met a fellow sailor, Steve, and we became very good friends. He invited me to join him on a sailing trip to the Bahamas aboard his sailboat *Retention*, and I agreed. I thought it would be nice, not being in charge for a change. Kia would accompany us, of course.

Steve was a skilled and conscientious captain. Knowing my history, he carefully monitored the weather and planned each leg of the trip according to prevailing conditions; every anchorage was a tranquil oasis. He did his job too well: my confidence was restored, and before long all I could think of was my boat languishing alone in Saint Augustine and what an amazing feeling it was to captain your own vessel. A crazy idea took shape in my mind. Maybe I could return to Saint Augustine and bring my boat over as well; we'd sail in tandem. Steve had some concerns, mostly about how long it would take. I promised three weeks at the most, and he agreed, saying he would watch Kia as well. And so I departed on my mission to bring *Gypsy Spirit* back to the islands.

My adventure started with the two day return trip to Saint Augustine, beginning with a sixty mile cab ride across Great Abaco to Grand Haven, then a high speed ferry, a bus, a cruise ship and finally a rental car. Once home I set a goal to depart in a week then worked from morning to night preparing the boat. Sails, engine, rigging, provisions, navigation, lights; I was leaving nothing to chance.

Departure day arrived; I drew in a deep breath and sailed out of the slip into the channel—alone. The sun was high, and clear skies were in the forecast as I motor-sailed south down the ditch. If all went well, I'd be ready to cross in several days. I'd arranged foodstuffs in the cockpit so that I wouldn't have to stop along the way: black beans and rice, peanut butter, bread, and water.

The days passed, pleasant though long and I found myself once again in West Palm Beach, preparing for the crossing. I needed fuel, so I brought the boat alongside the fuel dock and made arrangements to spend the night there. I was about to walk up to the shower room when all of the sudden I saw—Pirate Pete and Skippy.

"Hey there, stranger," I called out. Pete looked over but from a distance he didn't recognize me, then he looked toward my boat, and smiled.

"Howzit stranger? What are you doing here?"

"Hey, Pete," I said and ran over toward him. He wrapped me in a giant bear hug. "I'm heading to the Bahamas."

"Who's with you?"

"I'm solo. Do you think you are the only singlehanded sailor around?"

"Good for you, girl. I'm proud of you, and your boat—looks lekker, hey," he said nodding in approval.

"Thanks, Pete. It's really good to see you."

"Ya. When are you sailing?"

"I'll anchor out tomorrow and then leave the next morning."

We hugged again, and Pete said, "Come have dinner with me, we need to catch up."

"Sounds great, let me shower and I'll meet you at the Tiki Bar."

Two days later, I departed West Palm Beach with the rising sun; I raised the main, unfurled the jib, and sailed out the inlet toward the radiant sphere that was just barely peeking over the horizon. It was a quiet morning and *Gypsy Spirit* was a lone traveler on the open sea. I stood at the helm, hands upon the wheel, and looked out over the open expanse before me. I was ready for this...I'd known almost the moment I'd weighed anchor...This was my triumphant return to sailing. Gone were the demons of *could have*, *should have*, and *would have*; their questions had long since been answered, and my boat was no longer a mysterious conglomeration of unpredictable mechanical bits and fiberglass. It was a symphony of parts working in harmony (most of the time), and I was the conductor.

A couple of hours passed, I looked astern and watched as the West Palm skyline disappeared over the horizon. I set the autopilot and made my way toward the bow, climbed over the furler, and sat down on the bowsprit—my favorite spot. Legs dangling, hair blowing in the breeze, I inhaled the salt air, felt the caress of the wind and the soft kiss of the sun. I was master of my vessel...*Gypsy Spirit* and I—together in perfect harmony. We rose and fell on each gentle swell as the wind carried us forward. Pelicans flew overhead, and a pod of dolphins swam over to greet me. They leaped and dove through the undulating liquid blue caramel of the Gulf Stream. I stood and looked around—water and sky in every direction, just me and my tiny vessel out there upon the vast seemingly endless ocean—and I was filled with the most indescribable joy.

Maybe things would have turned out differently had I known that it was bad luck to rename a boat, but like I said: sometimes you just have to close your eyes, hold your breath, and jump—and that's what I did. I bought an old boat, christened her *Gypsy Spirit*, put my house on the market, and cajoled my reluctant fifty-pound mutt, Kia, into moving aboard...and I wouldn't change a thing.

Acknowledgements

Through adversity, I was given the opportunity to experience the best of humanity. I would like to thank my fellow cruisers and sailors, for without them there would be no story to tell. I'd especially like to thank; the captain and crew of *Mystic Gem*, who did everything they could to save Kia, me and my boat; Sean Pratt, Captain Etienne, Frankie, Jean Louis and Nino—the owner and the crew of the tugboat *Sussex*, who for no gain of their own, put time and energy into helping Gypsy Spirit and crew get to the Dominican Republic; Greg from Lagoon Keepers, who gave me an engine when we'd almost lost hope and helped keep the dream alive; Walter, who rebuilt my engine, not once but twice, even though he was "too old to be mucking around in the bilge of a sailboat"; Handy Andy, who watched over *Gypsy Spirit* while she was in the Dominican Republic; John Spires the owner of Oasis Boatyard, who made the boatyard a home; Nancy Beaudoin, whose friendship and moral support saw me through; Additionally I'd like to thank Pat Putnam for her emotional support and encouragement, Anne Edmunds for her insight and input, Amal Bukruian – my first reader, Sam, Pirate Pete, Lucky Mike, Clive, Susan Bradley and Gilda, Greg Russo, Dave Huff, Cindy and Vaughan Frye, Captain Joe, Rob and Beth, Stephen Ketchel, Marina Yapoujian and Ed of course, to name just a few people.

I would also like to acknowledge Kianda (Kia), a wise gentle soul and the best friend anyone could ask for.

I would like to thank my daughter Tanya and my father who both loved me enough to let me go. And most of all…I'd like to thank my Mother—for everything. I'd like to think that somehow she lived this adventure with me and that hers was the hand that carried the line to me on that dark and stormy night.

Appendix

Gypsy Spirit before collision

Rebuilding Gypsy Spirit

Gypsy Spirit sails again

Made in the USA
San Bernardino, CA
20 December 2013